TWO PLAYS FOR Y   ⌐ ıｌｅ

Phil Porter

TWO PLAYS FOR YOUNG PEOPLE

THE FLYING MACHINE
SMASHED EGGS

OBERON BOOKS
LONDON

First published in 2008 by Oberon Books Ltd
521 Caledonian Road, London N7 9RH
Tel: 020 7607 3637 / Fax: 020 7607 3629
e-mail: info@oberonbooks.com
www.oberonbooks.com

A catalogue record for this book is available from the British
Library.

ISBN: 978-1-84002-864-5

Cover illustration by Mark Oliver (courtesy of feastcreative.com)

Printed in Great Britain by CPI Antony Rowe, Chippenham.

Contents

THE FLYING MACHINE

Characters

NURSE CLARISSA CAKEBREAD

PEEKA CAVENDISH

MUNIB SIDDIQI

BONYEK STRANGLEMAN

SUPERINTENDENT KIMBERLEY RAINWATER (Voice of)

ROYSTON STRANGLEMAN (Ghost of)

The Flying Machine was first performed on 6 May 2008 at the Unicorn Theatre, London, with the following company:

NURSE CLARISSA CAKEBREAD, Maggie O'Brien

PEEKA CAVENDISH, Beverley Denim

MUNIB SIDDIQI / ROYSTON STRANGLEMAN,
    Daniel Naddafy

BONYEK STRANGLEMAN, Toyin Omari-Kinch

VOICE OF SUPERINTENDENT RAINWATER, Joanna David

All other parts were played by members of the company.

Director Rosamunde Hutt

Designer Jane Linz Roberts

Lighting Designer Nick MacLiammoir

Sound Designer Graeme Miller

Movement Lawrence Evans

Dramaturge Carl Miller

Company Stage Manager Emma Basilico

Deputy Stage Manager Helen Smith

Assistant Stage Manager Liam Clarke

SCENE ONE

(*The children's ward at St Ruth's Hospital For Damaged Eyes. Five iron beds lie in a line along the ward at equal distances apart.*

Beside each bed dangles a red 'alarm cord'. Also, each bed has a water tap sticking out of the wall beside it. A huge plug, about a metre in diameter, sits in a plughole in the centre of the room. It is attached to a chain which runs along the floor and up one wall to a lever. Next to that lever is another lever labelled 'sprinkler lever'.

A blackboard hangs on the wall. The words 'strorbreez', 'grayv' and 'muddd' have been chalked up on the board in chaotic and overlapping letters. There is just one window, very high up, and a window-opening pole. There is a boiler attached to the wall with a switch beside it. An old-fashioned green telephone sits on a little ledge on the wall. There is a large barrel marked 'Barrel Of Oddments'. The floor of the ward is dirty and the paint is flaking off the walls.

PEEKA and MUNIB are standing by their beds. They wear pyjamas. MUNIB's eyes are bandaged so he cannot see. PEEKA can see out of one eye – her other eye is covered with a dressing. NURSE CAKEBREAD stands near the door with BONYEK. She holds a clipboard.)

CAKEBREAD: Children, we have somebody new joining us. His name is Bonyek Strangleman. Say hello to them, Bonyek. (*Pause.*) Bonyek will be with us for quite some time, won't you, Bonyek? So, make him feel part of the family. Who would like to help Bonyek unpack his things?

PEEKA: I will, Nurse Cakebread.

CAKEBREAD: Peeka, thank you. And who would like to explain to Bonyek the way things work round here, all our little systems?

PEEKA: I will, Nurse Cakebread.

CAKEBREAD: Peeka. And who would like to be Bonyek's special settling-in friend?

MUNIB: I will, Nurse Cakebread.

CAKEBREAD: Peeka, would you do that for me? Thank you. Do you need the toilet, Bonyek? (*Pause.*) Well, I'm going to my office now, but if you do need anything, or if anything troubles you, just pull your alarm cord. There's one by every bed. I'll be back with your night-time medicines shortly.

(*NURSE CAKEBREAD leaves the ward. Pause.*)

PEEKA: Hello, Bonyek, my name's Peeka. Pleasure to have you aboard. (*Pause.*) Go on, Munib, tell him your name.

MUNIB: I'm Munib.

PEEKA: We've had our operations. You've got yours coming up, have you? Don't worry, you'll be fine. It's a grubby old hospital but the Visiting Surgeon has a good reputation.

(*BONYEK puts his case on one of the beds.*)

Ah…we're not allowed to touch Bed Number Four. It's okay, you weren't to know.

(*PEEKA picks up BONYEK's case, being careful not to touch the bed. She puts the case on a different bed.*)

I'd suggest this one. It's got the best remaining mattress.

MUNIB: Some have springs poking through, I'm afraid.

PEEKA: Let's see about unpacking this case. Get you nice and settled in.

(*PEEKA sets BONYEK's case down on the middle bed. She opens the case. It contains a spanner, two shoes and two bags of quick-drying cement.*)

Is that all you've got? One spanner, one shoe and two bags of quick-drying cement?

(*She closes the case and puts it at the foot of BONYEK's bed.*)

Well, everything you need's provided. Toothbrush, blankets, sheets… Oh, and there's a flannel and towel in the bedside drawer /

MUNIB: The flannels smell quite milky, I'm afraid.

PEEKA: Munib says the flannels smell milky but that's just him. He's got a very sensitive nose. Not so noticeable for the likes of us. (*Pause.*) What else? Instead of saying 'brilliant' we say 'grilliant' so look out for that. Oh, and there's a sprinkler system, look. They use it to clean the place.

MUNIB: Which happens hardly ever.

PEEKA: That's what the plug's for, they pull it out to stop the ward filling up with water. (*Pause.*) As far as entertainment goes, we spend most of our time on our projects, don't we, Munib? I'm making a town from all the dust and fluff that gathers round the edges of the room, look. I call it Fluffborough.

(*PEEKA produces a big chipboard rectangle. On it is a town made from dust and fluff.*)

I used Munib's hair for the railway lines, but apart from that it's all dust and fluff. Cathedral, office block, prison for the prisoners… (*Pause.*) Munib, tell Bonyek about your projects, you know I hate doing all the talking.

MUNIB: Well /

PEEKA: Munib does two projects, origami and The Register Of Smells. He's actually very able. Go on, Munib, tell Bonyek.

MUNIB: I do The Register Of Smells and origami, which means folding up paper into shapes. So far I've done a frog, two birds and a protoceratops.

(*PEEKA produces a board with an origami frog, two origami birds and an enormous origami protoceratops on it – a massive project perfectly executed.*)

Protoceratops means 'early horned face'. It took a long time to make because I can't see anything. (*Pause.*) My other project's The Register Of Smells. If I can smell something I write it on the blackboard.

(*MUNIB points somewhere other than the blackboard. PEEKA adjusts his arm.*)

Then Peeka copies it up in the exercise book before bed. So far today I've smelled strawberries, gravy and mud. (*Pause.*) Peeka.

PEEKA: Yes, Munib.

MUNIB: Is there really a boy called Bonyek?

PEEKA: Of course there is.

MUNIB: So why doesn't he speak?

BONYEK: 'Don't say a word till you've sized people up a bit.' That's my brother Royston's motto.

MUNIB: Was that Bonyek?

PEEKA: Yes, that was him.

BONYEK: But you two seem all right to me, in a weirdo kind of way.

PEEKA: Thank you, I think.

BONYEK: No probs. So what kind of stuff do you do for fun round here?

PEEKA: For fun?

BONYEK: Yeah, for like fun. What kind of stuff do you do?

PEEKA: Like I was saying, I'm making a town from /

BONYEK: Yeah, but what about actual fun?

PEEKA: I don't understand.

BONYEK: Like when Cakebread snoozes off or whatever.

MUNIB: I think he means things like…adventures.

BONYEK: Yeah, stuff like that, what do you do for fun?

(*Pause as MUNIB and PEEKA think about this.*)

PEEKA: Well… We… Sometimes we talk about boats.

BONYEK: You talk about boats?

MUNIB: Peeka knows all about them from books.

BONYEK: Yeah, talking about boats ain't an adventure.

PEEKA: Well, no, but /

BONYEK: Being on a boat, an actual one, now that's a whole different kettle of spanners /

PEEKA: Yes, well, sadly, Bonyek, we don't have any actual boats on the ward. Or rivers or lakes or oceans. So actual boating isn't actually much of an option.

BONYEK: I don't know about that.

(*BONYEK grabs the large wooden window-opening pole.*)

PEEKA: Er…what are you doing?

BONYEK: Just cos we ain't got no real boats, don't mean we can't have a kind of adventure. (*He slots the pole into the frame of MUNIB's bed to create a mast.*) There. One mast.

PEEKA: Actually, no, I don't think that's a very good idea.

BONYEK: Why not?

PEEKA: Well, for one thing, Nurse Cakebread will be back soon.

BONYEK: So? 'No fun without danger' my brother Royston always says.

PEEKA: Royston never met Nurse Cakebread /

BONYEK: (*Attaching a sheet to the pole.*) One sail.

PEEKA: Please don't do that /

BONYEK: In the mood for a voyage, Munib?

PEEKA: Come away, Munib.

MUNIB: (*Gripping the makeshift mast.*) A voyage to where?

PEEKA: Munib, come away.

BONYEK: Anywhere you like. Over rapids, out to sea, down some kind of African river with hippos and all that kind of stuff…

MUNIB: Out to sea!

BONYEK: (*Climbs aboard.*) Out to sea it is then.

MUNIB: This is going to be grilliant. Totally, utterly grilliant.

BONYEK: Okay, before we get going, best check we've got all the stuff. Mast.

MUNIB: Check.

BONYEK: Sail.

MUNIB: Check.

PEEKA: This is so babyish.

BONYEK: Rations.

MUNIB: Rations?

BONYEK: Hang about, I've got the rations. I made them before I came.

(*BONYEK takes some sandwiches wrapped in foil from his pocket and waves them in front of MUNIB's face.*)

MUNIB: Mmm, chicken and beetroot, my favourite.

BONYEK: So...

(*As BONYEK describes the scene the environment changes. The boat is isolated by a blue and blissful wave-reflected light. The sheet becomes taut like a sail. Gulls make gull noises. The bedboat rocks gently. PEEKA looks on jealously.*)

...first we imagine the smell of the sea, all salty and fishy and stuff. Then we imagine the feel of the air on our skin, and the sound of the wind in the sail, and the sound of the seagulls and the... Hang on a tick.

(*Snap back to reality.*)

MUNIB: What?

BONYEK: There's something we forgot. We need a Captain. Someone to be first-in-command and order us about and that kind of stuff. Someone that knows about boats.

MUNIB: Peeka knows about boats.

BONYEK: Yeah, but Peeka thinks it's babyish.

PEEKA: I don't think it's...completely babyish.

BONYEK: What, you mean you'll be Captain?

PEEKA: If it'll help you out...

MUNIB: Grilliant.

BONYEK: Jump aboard, Skip. No time to lose. We've got a big voyage ahead.

(*PEEKA boards the bedboat. We return to the blissful ocean environment as BONYEK describes the scene.*)

So, the taste of the air. And the way it feels on our skin. The smell of the sea and the seagulls making noises and stuff. And the wind in the sail and the sound of the waves going like blonk-blonk against the side of the boat.

MUNIB: What's the weather like?

BONYEK: Can't you feel it? It's kind of hot but there's kind of like a breeze?

MUNIB: Oh yeah, I can feel it now. It's kind of…hot, but kind of…breezy!

BONYEK: Not many clouds.

MUNIB: And what's it called, the boat?

BONYEK: Don't ask me, ask the Skip.

MUNIB: What's it called, Peeka?

PEEKA: Call me Skipper.

MUNIB: What's it called, Skipper?

PEEKA: She's called Pilgrim Nine and she's a sloop. That means one sail. But we're not here to talk amongst ourselves, we're here to feed the hungry dolphins.

(*The clicking and giggling of dolphins surrounds the bedboat.*)

MUNIB: Dolphins!

PEEKA: There's less and less fish in this part of the sea, that's why they're getting a bit hungry.

(*PEEKA distributes imaginary buckets of fish…*)

Munib, you take the mackerel. Bonyek, take the sticklebacks. I'll take the blueback sprats. They're very hungry, so feed them as much as they'll eat.

(*They feed the imaginary dolphins with fish from the imaginary buckets. The dolphins splash and chirrup gratefully.*)

MUNIB: They love it, they're snatching the mackerels right out of my hand!

BONYEK: Here you go, old boy. Munch on that. Loads more where that came from.

PEEKA: Don't be afraid to give them two at once. It really is a matter of stuffing them till they almost burst.

MUNIB: Here you go, dolphin. Swallow that down. Nice and lovely.

BONYEK: Look!

PEEKA: What?

BONYEK: There!

MUNIB: Where?

BONYEK: I think it's a...!

(*BONYEK points MUNIB's arm to a spot in the water to one side of the bedboat.*)

It's a killer whale! And it's going to jump right over the boat!

(*There is a rumbling, whooshing noise as the imaginary animal launches itself out of the water. They follow it as it flies over the boat, BONYEK guiding MUNIB's arm to chart the animal's trajectory. Eventually, the whale lands in the water with an almighty crash.*)

MUNIB: Wow! That was so majestic! I don't think I've ever seen anything better! Or more majestic!

PEEKA: Uh oh.

BONYEK: What is it, Skip?

PEEKA: (*Sucks her finger and holds it up.*) The weather's taking a turn for the worse. I think there's a storm a-brewin'.

(*The bedboat begins to lurch and pitch as the sky darkens and the wind picks up. Imaginary rain hammers down in golf-ball drops...*)

MUNIB: I don't like it. I don't like all the rain!

PEEKA: All right, Munib, just do as I say and we'll be fine.

MUNIB: It's getting down my vest and pants!

PEEKA: Munib, take down the sail! Bonyek, grab the rudder! We must face into the breaking waves or we'll capsize!

(*MUNIB and BONYEK set about their tasks. PEEKA looks through imaginary binoculars. The weather continues to worsen.*)

BONYEK: How's it looking, Skipper?!

PEEKA: Not good! It's a force ten and it's heading this way!

BONYEK: She won't turn!

PEEKA: Keep trying, Bonyek! It's coming from the east!

MUNIB: (*At the top of the pole.*) I can't do it! It's all snagged up!

PEEKA: It's all right, Munib! I'm coming!

(*PEEKA helps MUNIB to release the sheet.*)

BONYEK: Look out!

(An imaginary wave crashes into the side of the bedboat. MUNIB screams. Their voices can barely be heard above the roar of the storm.)

PEEKA: Scramble to the high side!

(They cling to one side of the bedboat, only their weight preventing a capsize. Another wave crashes into the vessel, sending them sprawling.)

PEEKA: Cling on!

MUNIB: I can't!

PEEKA: For dear life!

MUNIB: It's too strong!

BONYEK: *(Points.)* Tidal wave!

PEEKA: What?!

BONYEK: Tidal wave!!!

(A massive wave hits the bedboat. PEEKA, BONYEK and MUNIB can cling on no longer and they are thrown from the bedboat. The sound of the mighty storm disappears and is replaced by the sound of cicadas, far-away elephants and gentle waves nudging pebbles back and forth on a stony beach. The sun is setting. The children cough and splutter and crawl about. MUNIB and BONYEK crawl into one another. They feel each other's faces…)

MUNIB: Where are we?

BONYEK: I don't know. It's all sand and stuff. Must be some kind of desert island.

MUNIB: Are we alive?

BONYEK: I reckon.

PEEKA: We are alive. Father Neptune, God of the sea, has brought us to the island of Habbagoogaloogaloo, a place full of diamonds and wild pigs. We will live here for the rest of our days. Munib, sniff out some supper with your excellent nose. Bonyek, build a shack with three hammocks and a separate changing area for girls. I'll start a fire by rubbing a stick with another stick /

CAKEBREAD: What's this, a game of Let's Pretend?

PEEKA: Nurse Cakebread!

(*The desert island sounds disappear and the light returns to normal. NURSE CAKEBREAD is standing with a tray of medicines, having returned to the ward unnoticed. PEEKA and MUNIB rush to stand beside their beds.*)

CAKEBREAD: It's certainly a messy game, whatever it is. I was only away a short time.

(*NURSE CAKEBREAD gives PEEKA pills and some water. She swallows the pills.*)

It's not like you, Peeka Cavendish. To be playing at dangerous games. And talking about rubbing sticks with other sticks. There are few enough good eyes on the ward without us wafting the window-opening pole hither and thither, don't you think?

PEEKA: Yes, Nurse Cakebread. Sorry, Nurse Cakebread.

(*NURSE CAKEBREAD spoons gloopy medicine into MUNIB's mouth…*)

CAKEBREAD: Nurse Cakebread goes out of her way to make your time here happy, Munib. She battled long and hard with all three Boards of Governors to get the paper for your paper-folding. And the chalk for your Register Of Smells. Dragging her fresh today sheets across the floor seems a little ungrateful.

MUNIB: Sorry, Nurse Cakebread.

(*NURSE CAKEBREAD turns to BONYEK.*)

Lie down, Bonyek.

(*Pause. BONYEK lies on his bed.*)

Good boy.

(*NURSE CAKEBREAD administers eyedrops…*)

It's natural that you should feel unsettled, Bonyek. New places and new people can be frightening. But try not to be an Unsettler Of Others. Here at St Ruth's we have a motto, don't we children? And what is it?

MUNIB: 'Pietas famulatus veneratio'.

CAKEBREAD: That's right, Peeka. And what does 'pietas famulatus veneratio' mean?

MUNIB: It means 'kindness obedience respect'.

CAKEBREAD: That's right, Peeka. And what do we mean by 'respect'? When we say respect, what do we mean?

MUNIB: Being polite?

CAKEBREAD: No, Munib, we don't mean 'being polite'. We mean 'not being an Unsettler Of Others'. 'Pietas famulatus veneratio'. We'll have four hours of project time before bed. Bonyek, your project is to find a project. Something calm with no unsettlingness. You can look in the Barrel Of Oddments for inspiration.

(*NURSE CAKEBREAD points out the Barrel Of Oddments and heads for the door.*)

Oh, I almost forgot… As a reward for all her hard work, Nurse Cakebread has been granted a week's holiday, starting tomorrow. And she's chosen to return to the beautiful Greek island of Zakynthos.

PEEKA: You mean…you won't be here?

CAKEBREAD: Don't get too upset. Nurse Cakebread's sister-in-law will fill in while she's away, and her name is also Nurse Cakebread, and she's exactly as nice as I am. And when I come back, those of you that can see can look at my photographs. So that's something to look forward to, isn't it?

PEEKA: Yes, Nurse Cakebread.

(*Again NURSE CAKEBREAD heads for the door, but she is distracted by the protoceratops.*)

CAKEBREAD: Munib, you finished your protoceratops! How splendid!

MUNIB: Thank you, Nurse Cakebread.

CAKEBREAD: I shall miss you when I'm away. I shall miss you all.

(*NURSE CAKEBREAD goes. PEEKA gets to work on Fluffborough. BONYEK sits on the end of his bed. MUNIB gets back on his hands and knees, continuing his search for food on Habbagoogaloogaloo.*)

MUNIB: Parsnips! There's parsnips, buried in the soil, I can smell them! (*He digs at the imaginary soil with his hands.*) Oh yes indeedy, these'll roast up a treat. How's that fire coming along, Skip?

PEEKA: What fire?

MUNIB: (*Pulling imaginary parsnips from the ground.*) The one you were starting. We need it for the roasting up of these little beauties.

PEEKA: Munib, your hand is empty. There are no parsnips. There is no Habbagoogaloogaloo, I made it up. It's all just a silly, stupid, made-up bag of animal poo!

MUNIB: But Peeka /

PEEKA: No, I don't want to play. It's not real and it got us in trouble with Nurse Cakebread.

MUNIB: Who cares about Nurse Cakebread? I don't.

PEEKA: You were pleased enough when she called your protoceratops splendid, Munib Siddiqi.

(*PEEKA resumes work on her dust-and-fluff town.*)

MUNIB: What about you, Bonyek? Fancy cooking up some parsnips under the stars?

BONYEK: Nah.

MUNIB: Oh but go on. It's amazing the way you made us think it was real.

BONYEK: Nah, Peeka was right in the first place. I mean, doing stuff for pretend's kind of okayish. But it's kind of babyish too when you think about it and stuff.

PEEKA: Precisely.

BONYEK: Cos what's the point? You finish playing and you're back in the same old stupid world. How's that worth getting in trouble for?

PEEKA: Precisely. Well said, Bonyek.

BONYEK: Cos why do pretend adventures when we could just as easy bust out of this place and go on a real one? With actual real danger and real actual stuff happening?

PEEKA: That's precisely what I'm saying. No it isn't.

BONYEK: Come here, Munib. I got something to show you.

PEEKA: (*As MUNIB stumbles over to BONYEK.*) Bonyek, tell me
you're not serious about breaking out.

(*BONYEK picks up his suitcase…*)

Listen, I know it's not easy being cooped up… But
escaping? We're here because we need to be here /

BONYEK: One perfectly normal suitcase, right, Munib?

MUNIB: I don't know, I can't see.

BONYEK: Wrong. For here we have a secret compartment.
(*He reveals the secret compartment.*) And what should the
secret compartment have inside it?

(*BONYEK produces a big, tatty map. It is drawn in pencil with
blue annotations and red crosses marking certain areas.*)

Oh look! If it's not a whole big massive map of St Ruth's
Hospital For Damaged Eyes!

MUNIB: Wow!

PEEKA: Where did you get that map?

(*BONYEK dances jubilantly around PEEKA with the map and
sings. MUNIB is very excited by the map and the map song…*)

BONYEK: (*To the tune of 'Where Did You Get That Hat?'.*) 'Where
did you get that map?

Where did you get that map?'

PEEKA: I demand to know where you got it from!

BONYEK: Isn't it a lovely map?

And just the proper kind of map?

PEEKA: Bonyek, please, I don't like any of this /

BONYEK: Right, let's whack this on the wall. Have a good old
squizzle. Let the monkey see the rabbit!

(*BONYEK sticks the map over the Register Of Smells.*)

PEEKA: Careful!

BONYEK: What of?

PEEKA: The Register Of Smells, I haven't copied it up yet.

MUNIB: Who cares? I don't.

BONYEK: So! She's in bits at the moment, she was too big to hide in one piece. (*He points at the various red crosses.*) There's a big bit behind the shed, some stuff behind the dustbins, stuff up this tree… I reckon we drag it all to here, it's a garden with like walls all round it, and that's where we stick it all together. Any questions?

PEEKA: I have a question.

BONYEK: Yeah?

PEEKA: Well, apart from knowing you're being stupid and dangerous, I don't actually understand what you're talking about. Bits of what? Stick what together?

BONYEK: What, didn't I say?

PEEKA: No.

BONYEK: It's a flying machine!

(*BONYEK tugs on the map and it unfurls to reveal a flying machine design.*)

MUNIB: A flying machine?!

BONYEK: Yeah. It's in pieces at the moment.

MUNIB: A flying machine?!

BONYEK: Yeah. They're hidden round the grounds of the hospital.

MUNIB: A flying machine?!

BONYEK: Yeah. It's my brother Royston's. He was in here last year. What he did, he sneaked out every night, built all the bits and hid them round the gardens. He was going to fly it too, with his mates, Inky and Blocker.

MUNIB: So why didn't he?

BONYEK: Got caught sneaking out, didn't they? Then Cakebread wouldn't leave the ward. She even slept in here, so they never got to fly it. So we're going to fly it instead.

MUNIB: That is the utterly most grilliant story I ever heard.

BONYEK: Yeah, 'cept it ain't just a story, it's true. So, who's with me?

MUNIB: Me. Definitely, absolutely, one million per cent.

BONYEK: Peeka?

PEEKA: No. I don't want anything to do with it. And I don't think you should either, Munib.

MUNIB: (*Spinning around, arms out like wings.*) It'll be grilliant! We'll fly like actual birds!

PEEKA: (*Stops MUNIB.*) But what if we get caught like they did? We'll have our privileges taken away.

BONYEK: What privileges?

PEEKA: Every Sunday we get to share a slice of cheese on toast. Every Wednesday we get to use normal toothpaste. And now there's holiday photographs to think about...

BONYEK: Who cares about holiday photographs? It's just a load of fat, red legs and drinks with umbrellas /

PEEKA: And what about The Minute Of Air?

BONYEK: What's The Minute Of Air?

MUNIB: At three o'clock every day, for one minute, the roof disappears. It's almost time now...

PEEKA: You get to taste the air and look up at the sky. It's the best part of the day. If we get caught, they'll switch it off.

MUNIB: (*To PEEKA.*) But this'll be like three hundred Minutes Of Air in a row. And we won't get caught, she's busy packing for her holiday.

BONYEK: And if we do get caught, I'll take the blame. So it'll be me she punishes. (*Pause.*) Come on, Skip, don't be frightened.

PEEKA: I'm not frightened, I just don't want to risk my privileges on something that won't work. I mean, did Royston have any actual...qualifications in aircraft design?

BONYEK: He was only eleven.

PEEKA: I just don't think it'll lift off the ground.

BONYEK: But imagine if it does!

MUNIB: (*Spinning round again.*) Imagine!

BONYEK: Over chimneys, over fields, harbours full of sailing boats and stuff. Swooping down and doing loop-the-loop /

PEEKA: I don't like being upside down. It's not natural.

BONYEK: Okay /

PEEKA: I'd rather just fly nice and straight.

BONYEK: Okay, we'll fly nice and straight and go wherever you want. If you could fly anywhere, where would it be?

PEEKA: Well…

BONYEK: Anywhere. America, Brazil…

MUNIB: (*Spinning around.*) Anywhere!

BONYEK: The North Pole, Australia, Brazil…

PEEKA: Well, if I did come… And if it did work…

BONYEK: Yeah?

PEEKA: I'd want to go home and find the answer to The Mystery.

BONYEK: What mystery?

PEEKA: Of why they don't visit any more.

MUNIB: We call it The Mystery.

PEEKA: They came every day. My mum, Munib's mum and sometimes Munib's dad.

MUNIB: My dad works funny hours at the sauce factory.

PEEKA: But then they stopped. Without warning. Fifty-four days ago.

BONYEK: (*Writes on the plan.*) Okay. First stop, Peeka's house.

PEEKA: But I didn't say /

MUNIB: Then can we go to mine? So I can ask mine too.

BONYEK: (*Writes on the plan.*) Okay, second stop, Munib's house. Third stop, my choice, Brazil. So, are we agreed?

MUNIB: Agreed.

BONYEK: Peeka?

PEEKA: I don't know…

BONYEK: Oh, go on.

MUNIB: Yeah, go on, Peeks. Then The Mystery won't be a mystery.

PEEKA: I just don't think it'll lift off the ground.

BONYEK: But that's the thing, it probably won't if you don't come. Look, three sets of pedals. (*He points at the diagram.*)

(*Pause.*)

PEEKA: All right, but /

MUNIB: Yessssssssssssssssssssssssssssssssssssssss.

PEEKA: But we have to be back in plenty of time. I can't lose my privileges. Especially not the cheese on toast, I can barely even think about it.

BONYEK: Okay, that leaves us with just one problem. How to get out of the building. (*Points at map.*) Best exit's here. That means sneaking past Adult Ward Two and the security office /

PEEKA: Easy. Munib, make three coats from white paper. We'll pretend to be doctors. I'll make some false beards with my dust and fluff supply.

MUNIB: But you were saving that to finish the fire station.

PEEKA: The firemen of Fluffborough will have to wait for their games room. It won't take long to gather some more. If there's one thing this world won't ever run out of it's fluff.

BONYEK: Okay, come here, everyone. (*They gather.*) Gob on your hand and whack it in the middle.

MUNIB and BONYEK spit enthusiastically onto their palms and put them in the middle. PEEKA daintily licks her palm with the very tip of her tongue and puts her hand in.

BONYEK: When I turned up, I didn't know who they'd put me in with. They could have whacked me in with any old bumheads. But I got well lucky. You two got what it takes to make this one totally good adventure, I reckon.

(*A loud buzzing noise.*)

What's that?

PEEKA: The Minute Of Air.

(*The roof retracts, filling the ward with sunshine and birdsong. They look up at the sky.*)

BONYEK: Wow. That's well nice. Wow. I've never seen the sky that blue before. (*Pause.*) Okay, give me your hands.

(*MUNIB adds some more spit for good measure. They put their hands in the middle again…*)

Repeat after me.

(*PEEKA and MUNIB repeat each line of the following oath…*)

We vow.

To be loyal.

To the project.

And each other.

Not do nothing silly and stuff.

And keep things secret.

Or else.

(*A solemn pause. Another buzz. The sunlight and birdsong disappear as they withdraw their hands and go about their business.*)

Okay, time is precious. Munib, get cracking on the uniforms. Make them nice and wide. We need to smuggle the bags of cement out.

PEEKA: Why?

BONYEK: They hang from the sides to help it balance.

MUNIB: Right-o!

BONYEK: Peeka, get on with the beards. I'll study the plans and stuff.

(*MUNIB and PEEKA set to work.*)

I'm telling you, this is going to be grilliant.

(*BONYEK studies and annotates the diagrams and plans. Scene ends.*)

SCENE TWO

(*The walled garden at St Ruth's Hospital For Damaged Eyes. A grassy area with a scorched circle at its centre. It is night-time but the area is lit, albeit dimly, by the moon, by the stars, by light shining out from the windows of the hospital and by the lamp-posts that line the nearby driveway. BONYEK dashes into the walled garden dressed in his false beard and origami white coat. He calls out in a whisper...*)

BONYEK: Hurry up!

(*PEEKA arrives, leading MUNIB by the hand. They both wear false beards and paper coats. PEEKA is anxious. MUNIB is wobbly with excitement and wonder. BONYEK lays the building plans out on the ground...*)

MUNIB: I can smell cars, I can smell...the sauce factory, I can smell...frozen grass /

BONYEK: Okay, does everyone remember the plan? Me and Peeka do the fetching and slotting together. Munib, you're in charge of tightening stuff that needs tightening and loosening stuff that needs loosening... (*BONYEK puts a spanner in MUNIB's hand.*)

PEEKA: Bonyek, I don't think this is such a grilliant idea. What if he suspected something.

BONYEK: Who?

PEEKA: The security man. He asked if Munib was a real doctor.

BONYEK: Did he? What did you say Munib?

MUNIB: I just said 'pietas famulatus veneratio'.

BONYEK: And what did he say?

MUNIB: He just said 'fair enough' and carried on eating his soup. Celery soup if I'm not mistaken.

BONYEK: Then we're fine. If he suspected us, he wouldn't have let us past. And anyway, why would he suspect us? These beards are grilliant. (*PEEKA is unconvinced.*) Okay, I'll fetch the main section, it's behind the groundsman's shed. Peeka, get the wings. They're over there in those dark bushes.

(*BONYEK heads for the groundsman's shed. PEEKA grabs MUNIB and tries to lead him away. He doesn't want to go.*)

PEEKA: I'll take you back in.

MUNIB: Back in? Why?

PEEKA: Because you're frightened.

MUNIB: I'm not. I love it out here. I can feel the breeze on the backs of my ears.

(*MUNIB pulls free of PEEKA.*)

Hey, you know I couldn't think what your mum smells like. I've got it. Raspberry sauce from ice cream vans. Doesn't she?

PEEKA: (*A lie.*) No.

MUNIB: She does. Just think, in two hours you could be sitting on the sofa, squashed right up close to your mum, the smell of raspberry sauce filling your nose.

PEEKA: Yeah, except it won't happen, will it?! Because they've probably moved away without telling us, haven't they?!

MUNIB: No.

PEEKA: So, why don't they visit any more, idiot?!

MUNIB: All right, I'm only trying to cheer you up cos you're scared.

PEEKA: I'm not scared.

MUNIB: You are, Peeka, you're well scared.

PEEKA: I'm not, and stop talking like Bonyek.

MUNIB: I ain't talking like no-one.

PEEKA: Stop it. It sounds stupid from your mouth.

MUNIB: It's okay to be frightened.

PEEKA: Good, fine, but I'm not.

MUNIB: But you are.

PEEKA: If anyone's scared, it's you.

MUNIB: I'm not scared.

PEEKA: Well, neither am I.

MUNIB: Well, you sound it.

PEEKA: Well, I'm not.

MUNIB: Well, neither am I.

PEEKA: Good.

MUNIB: I'm happy.

PEEKA: Good.

MUNIB: Darkness is my natural habitat.

PEEKA: Good then, fine, shut your mouldy mouth! (*Pause.*) Right. I'll fetch the wings from the dark bushes, shall I?

(*PEEKA heads off to fetch the wings. BONYEK returns, dragging the main section of the flying machine. It has three seats and three sets of pedals.*)

BONYEK: Pretty impressive, eh? So, if you get cracking with all the tightening and loosening, I'll go and get the figurehead.

(*BONYEK consults the map.*)

MUNIB: Bonyek. You know I'm in charge of tightening and loosening? Does that make me Head of it? Or are you Head of it and I'm just the person that's the worker?

BONYEK: (*As he walks off.*) You're more than just Head of it. You're Captain of it. Captain Of Tightening and Commander Of Loosening.

(*With enormous pride, MUNIB starts tightening and loosening parts of the machine. Each time he tightens something he says 'captain' to himself. Each time he loosens something he says 'commander'. PEEKA returns, dragging two enormous wings. She sets about slotting them into place.*)

(*Sniffs the air.*) Peeka?

PEEKA: What?

MUNIB: Guess what I am.

PEEKA: A very tiring little boy?

MUNIB: No, I'm Captain Of Loosening and Commander Of Tightening. No, Commander Of Loosening and Captain Of Tightening.

(*BONYEK returns with the figurehead – a large, rough sculpture of a bird's head stuck on the end of a pole. He slots the pole into the flying machine...*)

BONYEK: So, what about a name for it?

MUNIB: Yeah, what about a name for it?

BONYEK: Got to give it a name, else it's bad luck and stuff. Any suggestions?

MUNIB: What about Robert? I've always liked the name Robert.

BONYEK: Yeah, Robert's too much like a person's name. We need something a bit more...

MUNIB: What about...daffodil?

BONYEK: No, daffodil's too much like a flower. We need something a bit more...

MUNIB: Oh, oh, I've got it, oh, I've got it! (*Pause.*) Eskimo Soldier Two Nine One.

PEEKA: What about Firework?

BONYEK: Firework?

PEEKA: Yeah, Firework. Because fireworks fly, and that's a firebird's head and Munib and I are only here because fireworks blew up in our faces.

BONYEK: Firework. I like it. Firework it is then.

MUNIB: Firework! That's such a grilliant name! Peeka's always been grilliant at naming stuff! Like Pilgrim and Fluffborough /

PEEKA: Yes, all right, Munib, don't be a creep, I've already forgiven you for being stupid.

BONYEK: Oh...bum!

PEEKA: What is it?

BONYEK: Bum! Bum! Bum! Bum! Bum!

PEEKA: What is it, Bonyek?

BONYEK: We forgot the bags of cement.

MUNIB: Oh bum! Bum! Bum! Bum!

PEEKA: Does it make any difference?

BONYEK: It'll be harder to steer now.

PEEKA: At least it'll be lighter.

BONYEK: Yeah, but it's all about the wonkiness. Still, nothing we can do. It's too risky to go back. We've just got to hope it doesn't wreck everything. Come on, get to work.

(*Pause as BONYEK consults his plans and MUNIB and PEEKA work on Firework.*)

MUNIB: What do you think he'll say?

PEEKA: Who?

MUNIB: Royston, when he finds out we flew his machine.

(*Pause.*)

BONYEK: He won't say anything.

MUNIB: But he'll be pleased, won't he?

(*Pause.*)

BONYEK: Royston's dead.

MUNIB: What?

BONYEK: Royston's dead. He drowned. In the river. I tried to save him but it was too late. That's why I keep his shoe. To remember him by.

(*Pause.*)

PEEKA: I think he'll be pleased. I bet he's peeping down on us right now and smiling. And just wait till we get it flying. He'll be laughing so loud the others have to tell him to be quiet.

(*Scene ends.*)

SCENE THREE

(*NURSE CAKEBREAD's office. There is a messy desk and a chair on either side of it; one comfy, the other hard. On the desk is a large console with three levers and many buttons and flashing lights. Boxes and piles of paper sit on the floor around the desk and the walls are covered with charts. A CCTV monitor switches between several cameras, staying with each camera for ten seconds or so. There is also an unmade camp bed, a tatty lamp, an old radio and a makeshift dressing table.*)

NURSE CAKEBREAD is having a lovely time. Music comes from the radio as she packs her suitcase. The case is overflowing, but she continues to add items…)

CAKEBREAD: Sunglasses…foot lotion…swimming cap…

(She picks up a book.)

'A Violet Nosegay by Mariella Haberdash.'

(She kisses the book, puts it in the suitcase, closes the suitcase and sits on it to squash its contents down.)

Zakynthos here I come!

(She snaps the case shut. As she does so, the CCTV monitor switches to show Children's Ward One. It is empty. At first, she cannot believe her eyes. She gets up. She switches off the radio and presses a button to fix the monitor on the ward, then presses her face up close to the screen. She pulls a lever and a microphone descends. She speaks into it nervously…)

Children. Come out from under your beds. I repeat, come out from under your beds. Hiding under beds is a Grade Two offence.

(She stares at the screen. Nothing.)

Dammit!

(She pulls the second lever and a second microphone descends. NURSE CAKEBREAD speaks into it.)

Hello? Hello?

RAINWATER: *(Relayed through a speaker.)* Yes, Nurse Cakebread, what is it?

CAKEBREAD: Nurse Rainwater, we have a problem.

RAINWATER: I beg your pardon.

CAKEBREAD: *(Through gritted teeth.)* Superintendent Rainwater, we have a problem. The children are missing from Children's Ward One.

RAINWATER: Oh, not again.

CAKEBREAD: What do you mean?!

RAINWATER: You know what I mean. Just…hurry up and raise the alarm.

(*NURSE CAKEBREAD pulls the third lever. A howling siren sound begins and lights flash as a third microphone descends. NURSE CAKEBREAD speaks into it. Her words are relayed throughout the many filthy, echoing halls and wards of St Ruth's…*)

CAKEBREAD: Code purple. I repeat, code purple. Patients are missing from Children's Ward One. Commence search immediately. I repeat, commence search immediately.

(*The siren continues. Scene ends.*)

SCENE FOUR

(*BONYEK, PEEKA and MUNIB are busy tightening nuts, loosening bolts, slotting stuff into other stuff etc. They are all still wearing their beards. The construction work is nearly done. The siren can be heard in the distance. It continues through the scene…*)

MUNIB: What's that noise?

BONYEK: Code Purple.

PEEKA: What's a Code Purple?

BONYEK: Missing Patients Alarm. Cakebread must have must have looked in on the ward.

PEEKA: What?! Bonyek, you promised we wouldn't get caught!

BONYEK: Okay, just stay calm, yeah?

PEEKA: Stay calm?!

BONYEK: We've got five minutes max before they find us.

MUNIB: It's all going wrong.

PEEKA: (*Grabs MUNIB's hand.*) Come on, Munib, we're going back to the ward.

BONYEK: (*Blocks their path.*) Are you mad? Escaping's a Grade One Offence, the punishment's going to be way worse than no more cheese on toast and stuff.

PEEKA: It won't be as bad if we turn ourselves in.

BONYEK: Cakebread's a cow, she don't play by the rules.

PEEKA: Fine, so what do you suggest, Bonyek? What great plan have you got for us now?

MUNIB: It's all going wrong, I can smell it.

BONYEK: We stick to Plan A. The machine's pretty much done. We stop wasting time and start pedalling. Once we're in the sky, ain't nothing they can do. Got any strength in them legs, Munib?

MUNIB: They've gone a bit wobbly.

PEEKA: Bonyek, if you think it's going to fly, you're even more stupid than I already think you are.

BONYEK: It's got to be worth a try. And if we get caught, I take the blame, I already promised. And you promised to be loyal to the project.

PEEKA: I didn't promise, I vowed.

BONYEK: Same difference! I thought we were doing it for Royston.

(*Pause.*)

PEEKA: All right, but /

BONYEK: Grilliant, no time to lose. Which of you's the strongest?

MUNIB: She is, by miles.

BONYEK: Grilliant. Peeks, you sit here. You've got to pedal and row. (*PEEKA takes her place on the machine.*) I'll go the other side. Munib, you sit in the middle. (*He leads MUNIB to the central seat.*) You don't row but you've still got to pedal, yeah? And you've got to steer.

PEEKA: How can he steer? He can't see.

BONYEK: He'll be okay, we'll give him directions. The important thing is to get in the sky at all. Is everyone ready? Cos they'll be here any minute.

MUNIB: I'm ready.

PEEKA: Yes.

BONYEK: So, we get the speed going kind of slowly, yeah? All together, like one person that just happens to have six legs. Go.

(*They begin to pedal. Starting slowly, building up speed. The pedals cause the chopper blade to whizz around and whirr.*)

That's the stuff. Build it up slowly. One and two and three and four. Faster, faster, now with the wings.

(*BONYEK and PEEKA begin to move the wings up and down.*)

Up, down, up, down, faster, faster /

MUNIB: It's too difficult /

BONYEK: Keep going, Munib!

MUNIB: I don't know if I can /

BONYEK: Keep going! Faster, faster, faster, faster, faster, faster, faster!!!

(*A horrible grinding screech brings the pedalling and the whirring to a halt.*)

BONYEK: (*Climbs off the machine.*) Oh bum!

MUNIB: What happened?

BONYEK: The chain. It came off the thingy.

MUNIB: Is it broken?

BONYEK: I don't know. (*He checks the chain.*) No, it just came off the thingy. (*He puts the chain back on the thingy…*) Okay, that was nearly it, I reckon. I reckon we were like ten seconds from taking off, don't you reckon?

PEEKA: No.

BONYEK: 'Nothing never happens if you don't believe it's going to', that's what Royston used to say.

(*BONYEK is in his seat once more.*)

Ready, everyone?

MUNIB: Ready.

PEEKA: Ready.

BONYEK: All right.

(*Again, they pedal, starting slowly and building up speed. The blade whizzes and whirrs.*)

That's it. Faster. Faster. Wings. Faster, faster, keep going, don't stop /

MUNIB: I won't stop /

BONYEK: Keep going! Faster with the pedals! Faster with the wings!

(*A new sound builds, promising a take-off.*)

Harder!

MUNIB: It's getting lighter!

BONYEK: Harder!

PEEKA: Something's happening!

BONYEK: Yes! Yes! Yes! Yes! Yes! Yes! Yes! Yes! (*A new kind of grinding screech brings the machine to a sudden halt.*) No!

PEEKA: What happened?

BONYEK: The rotor blade. One of the nuts is loose, where's the spanner?

PEEKA: (*Points.*) Down there.

(*The spanner is on the ground. BONYEK grabs it and tightens a nut...*)

MUNIB: That was my fault. I failed in my duty.

BONYEK: Nobody's fault.

MUNIB: But I'm Captain Of Tightening.

BONYEK: We're a team. Everything bad is everyone's fault and everything good is thanks to everyone, okay?

(*BONYEK is back in position.*)

Okay. We nearly had her off the ground. This time we're going all the way.

CAKEBREAD: (*In the distance.*) Children!

PEEKA: Oh no...!

BONYEK: It's Cakebread, quick, pedal. (*Pause.*) Pedal!

(*They pedal furiously.*)

Faster.

MUNIB: She's going to find us.

CAKEBREAD: (*Getting closer.*) Children!

MUNIB: She's getting closer.

PEEKA: Wings!

(*They beat the wings.*)

MUNIB: She's going to kill us.

CAKEBREAD: (*Getting closer.*) Children!

BONYEK: We're going to fly, Munib.

PEEKA: Faster.

BONYEK: We're going to fly!

(*Firework lifts off the ground.*)

PEEKA: We're flying!

BONYEK: Keep going!

CAKEBREAD: (*Getting closer.*) Children!

MUNIB: I can feel it!

BONYEK: Keep going!

PEEKA: We're flying! We're really flying!!!

(*Another grinding screech grounds Firework with a crash.*)

BONYEK: No!!!

CAKEBREAD: (*Close by.*) Children!

PEEKA: What are we going to do?!

BONYEK: Run for it!

PEEKA: What?!

BONYEK: Run for it!

PEEKA: Where to?!

BONYEK: Anywhere, just follow me!

MUNIB: I can't!

BONYEK: You can, Munib!

MUNIB: No, my foot! It's stuck! It's all tangled up!

(*PEEKA and BONYEK run to MUNIB to release his foot.*)

PEEKA: Oh no…!

MUNIB: It's digging into my ankle…!

PEEKA: It's all right, Munib.

BONYEK: We have to go!

PEEKA: We're not going anywhere without Munib.

MUNIB: It hurts!

BONYEK: We're going to get caught!

PEEKA: You go then!

(*After a moment's indecision, BONYEK makes a run for it. PEEKA makes a last attempt to release MUNIB's foot before resigning to her fate…*)

It's no use. It's completely stuck.

(*NURSE CAKEBREAD enters the walled garden, still in her dressing gown. She sees that MUNIB's foot is stuck. She pulls it free and leads MUNIB and PEEKA back to the hospital building. Scene ends. Interval.*)

SCENE FIVE

(*The Ghost of ROYSTON STRANGLEMAN stands alone in the ward. His eyes are wide and alarming. His hair, skin and clothes are dripping wet. He wears only one shoe. We hear the sound of his drowning as he would have heard it – an ominous low-pitched gurgle when his head is below the surface of the water; panicked gasps for breath and desperate splashing in the brief moments that his head is above the surface.*

The Ghost of ROYSTON STRANGLEMAN disappears.)

SCENE SIX

(*MUNIB is kneeling on the floor at the foot of his bed in despair. Strewn before him are the pieces of coloured paper that were once his origami creations. They have been unfolded, scrumpled and ripped. In vain, he tries to smooth them out with his hands. Meanwhile, Fluffborough is disappearing up the nozzle of a vacuum cleaner operated by NURSE CAKEBREAD. PEEKA, still in her beard, looks on in horror, fighting the urge to cry. The last row of bungalows for the elderly disappears up the sucking tube. NURSE CAKEBREAD switches the vacuum cleaner off. She switches it back on again and vacuums the beard from PEEKA's face. She switches it off again.*)

CAKEBREAD: I took no pleasure whatsoever in doing that.

(*NURSE CAKEBREAD tidies the vacuum cleaner away.*)

MUNIB: Do we still get our privileges?

CAKEBREAD: I beg your pardon.

MUNIB: Our privileges?

CAKEBREAD: I shall give my sister-in-law clear instructions. No more cheese on toast. No more soft toilet paper. No more pillows, blankets or sheets to sleep on or under. And you will wear the itchy punishment pyjamas, made from the wirey hair of my wire-haired dog Sminkey, until further notice. I'm sorry but you give me no choice.

(*NURSE CAKEBREAD picks up the receiver of the green phone on the wall and speaks into it.*)

Joyce? It's Clarissa. Two sets of Category Nine pyjamas to Children's Ward One, thank you.

(*NURSE CAKEBREAD puts the phone down, switches off the boiler and strips the beds, putting pillows, sheets and blankets into an enormous laundry sack…*)

Bonyek has been found. Up a tree behind the lens grinding workshop. He seems to be making a habit of letting people down. Did he tell you what happened to his brother Royston?

MUNIB: He drowned.

CAKEBREAD: But did he tell you how he drowned? They were playing in the river. They ran into trouble and Royston couldn't swim. So, Bonyek grabbed a hanging branch with one hand and Royston with the other. But Bonyek soon got tired of Royston's splashing and spluttering, so he let him go.

MUNIB: Is that true?

CAKEBREAD: You can read it for yourself. (*She gives PEEKA a newspaper cutting.*)

PEEKA: (*Reads.*) 'Local Boy Lets Brother Drown.'

CAKEBREAD: When you've got Bonyek for a friend, who needs enemies?

(*NURSE CAKEBREAD takes the laundry sack away.*)

PEEKA: I told you. I told you a hundred times we shouldn't go with him. I knew he wasn't to be trusted, I knew it.

(*Scene ends.*)

SCENE SEVEN

(*NURSE CAKEBREAD's office. BONYEK is sitting in the hard chair. From his grimy cheeks and general dishevelment you would think he had been on the run for more than fifty-three minutes. His attention is caught by a letter on NURSE CAKEBREAD's messy desk. He picks it up and begins to read it. He hears NURSE CAKEBREAD approaching and puts the letter back, half-read. NURSE CAKEBREAD enters and sits opposite BONYEK. She smiles at him. Her manner is disconcertingly calm and friendly.*)

CAKEBREAD: Hello, Bonyek. Would you like a cushion?

BONYEK: What for?

CAKEBREAD: To sit on. (*Pause.*) Or a blanket if you're cold?

BONYEK: Can we please just get it over with please?

CAKEBREAD: Get what over with?

BONYEK: My punishment? What's it to be? A week locked up in the dirty clothes cupboard? With nothing to eat except black bananas?

CAKEBREAD: What are you talking about?

BONYEK: That's what you did to Royston on his first day. When you thought he'd stole your wordsearch book.

CAKEBREAD: Bonyek, I promise you, here at St Ruth's we don't lock our patients in the dirty clothes cupboard. No matter what they've done. (*Pause, BONYEK still distrusting.*) So, Royston told a few stories about his time at St Ruth's, did he?

BONYEK: Yes. He did.

CAKEBREAD: Well, sometimes when we tell each other stories we exaggerate… Do you know what exaggerate means?

BONYEK: Make bigger.

CAKEBREAD: Exactly. We make things bigger to make the story more interesting. And sometimes this means adding things in that didn't really happen at all.

BONYEK: You calling my brother a liar?

CAKEBREAD: No, I'm calling him an excellent storyteller. What's that in your hair?

BONYEK: Where?

CAKEBREAD: (*Points.*) There.

BONYEK: (*Finds a stray feather.*) It's a feather.

CAKEBREAD: Well get rid of it.

BONYEK: Must have /

CAKEBREAD: Now! Get rid of it! Now!

> (*BONYEK puts the feather in his pocket. NURSE CAKEBREAD regains her composure.*)

> Where was I?

BONYEK: You were going on about Royston?

CAKEBREAD: Yes. (*Pause.*) Royston and I did fall out. He was caught sneaking out of the ward with his friends. And as it was my ward, my promotion to Superintendent was cancelled, so I now take orders from Superintendent Rainwater, who I hate. And I'll always hold Royston responsible for that. (*Pause.*) But you're not Royston, you're Bonyek. (*Pause.*) Tell me, what can I do to make your life here better, Bonyek? Are there any special foods or comforts you've been missing?

BONYEK: What you playing at?

CAKEBREAD: Nothing.

BONYEK: You are, what you playing at?

CAKEBREAD: I'm not playing at anything. A happy family is an easy one to look after, that's all. Is there anything you'd like?

> (*Pause.*)

BONYEK: It…

CAKEBREAD: Yes?

BONYEK: I suppose…

CAKEBREAD: Yes?

BONYEK: What you playing at?

CAKEBREAD: Bonyek, please!

(*Pause.*)

BONYEK: Well… It might be good if there was a telly. In the ward? Cos you've got telly up here, so why not down there? And films to watch and all that kind of stuff.

CAKEBREAD: There's a reason we don't have television. We don't want patients to strain their eyes. But we could allow a couple of hours each day if it's something you'd enjoy. (*She makes a note.*) Television. Anything else?

BONYEK: I suppose…

CAKEBREAD: Yes?

BONYEK: Well, it's a bit nippy. Could you like whack the heating up a bit?

CAKEBREAD: (*Makes a note.*) Heating.

BONYEK: And the mattresses have got all springs poking up through them and stuff.

CAKEBREAD: (*Makes a note.*) New mattresses.

BONYEK: And the sheets are plastic but I ain't going to wet myself and neither's Munib or Peeka, so why are they plastic?

CAKEBREAD: (*Makes a note.*) I'll look into borrowing some cotton bedsheets from Adult Ward One.

BONYEK: And what about the food? Munib says it's kind of sludgy and tastes like a kind of ointment taste.

CAKEBREAD: What would you like to eat?

BONYEK: I don't know. Stuff like…chicken and vegetable pie? Or…like…fish in breadcrumbs?

CAKEBREAD: (*Still making notes…*) Bread…crumbs…

BONYEK: And stuff like crisps?

CAKEBREAD: Crisps.

BONYEK: And I quite like grated carrots.

CAKEBREAD: Carrots…brackets…grated.

BONYEK: And ice cream.

CAKEBREAD: Chocolate? Strawberry?

BONYEK: Coconut.

CAKEBREAD: Co. Co. Nut.

(*Pause.*)

BONYEK: So is that what's going to happen? Telly and nice food and stuff?

CAKEBREAD: Yes, I can arrange those things immediately. But first I want you to promise me something.

BONYEK: What?

(*Pause.*)

CAKEBREAD: That you'll be my friend.

(*Pause.*)

BONYEK: Eh? What you playing at?

CAKEBREAD: I'm not playing at anything. I want you to be my friend.

(*NURSE CAKEBREAD offers her hand in friendship. BONYEK does not shake it.*)

Fine. Have it your way.

(*NURSE CAKEBREAD leads BONYEK away. Scene ends.*)

SCENE EIGHT

(*The ward. MUNIB and PEEKA are sitting in silence, still reeling from the events of the day. They are wearing the itchy doggy pyjamas. NURSE CAKEBREAD leads BONYEK into the room.*)

CAKEBREAD: Here he is. The Unsettler Of Others responsible for the end of your projects and the loss of your privileges.

(*She leads BONYEK to Bed Number Four.*)

Bonyek will be staying in Bed Number Four.

(*NURSE CAKEBREAD pulls the covers back and pushes BONYEK onto the bed. BONYEK lies on his back. There are straps attached to the sides of the bed. NURSE CAKEBREAD straps BONYEK in so he cannot move his arms or legs…*)

He will remain in Bed Number Four throughout his operation and until Nurse Cakebread returns from her holiday. And woebetide anyone that even thinks about loosening these straps, do I make myself clear?

PEEKA: Yes, Nurse Cakebread.

CAKEBREAD: (*Bandaging BONYEK's eyes.*) This is a preparation bandage, Bonyek. If you take it off before the operation, the operation won't work.

(*NURSE CAKEBREAD pulls a lever three times. Each time she pulls the lever there is a loud honking noise and the head of the bed lifts a few degrees.*)

(*One word after each honk.*) Pietas. Famulatus. Veneratio.

(*NURSE CAKEBREAD is about to leave the room. She stops.*)

CAKEBREAD: I'm not horrible. You don't think I'm horrible, do you, Peeka?

PEEKA: No, Nurse Cakebread.

CAKEBREAD: I'm under such a lot of pressure, that's all. From Superintendent Rainwater. That's not her real name, her real name's Kimberley. She's jealous of my looks so she bullies me. I'm not horrible.

(*Pause.*)

PEEKA: Nurse Cakebread. Do we have to wear the pyjamas? Only they're even more itchy than you think.

(*NURSE CAKEBREAD approaches PEEKA. She kisses her cheek.*)

CAKEBREAD: Only for a week. (*She takes out a large key.*) And I'm going to lock the door as well. Which is against the fire regulations but necessary under the circumstances.

(*NURSE CAKEBREAD goes, locking the door with a key.*)

BONYEK: Has she gone?

PEEKA: Yes.

BONYEK: About time. Weird or what? Loosen these straps. They're digging in like mental, I can't hardly breathe.

(*MUNIB and PEEKA stay put.*)

Yeah, second thoughts, you might be right. We're in enough trouble already, I reckon. (*Pause.*) Still, nothing to stop us using our imaginations. That dolphin feeding thing was all right, I reckon. Everyone lie down and I'll make up

46

a whole nother adventure, yeah? And we'll imagine it from our beds.

(*MUNIB and PEEKA are not lying down. They do not want to play. But as BONYEK speaks, the environment becomes real around them, just as it did for the dolphin-feeding expedition.*)

Okay, so we're walking through a kind of forest, and the birds are warbling in their nests, and it's first thing in the morning. And there's wispy mist like old men's beards all clinging off the branches. And we've got spears, yeah? Because there's going to be a fight. And we can hear the enemy close by, banging their drums and blowing their trumpets, and it's scary, but we grit our teeth and keep marching /

MUNIB: For we are warriors! Brave warriors that know no fear!

PEEKA: Munib, don't join in!

(*The environment snaps back to normal.*)

MUNIB: Sorry. He's just so grilliant at making me imagine things.

PEEKA: I don't care, we're not speaking to him, we agreed.

BONYEK: Eh?

PEEKA: He left you with your foot stuck, remember? He acts like the god of the world, and somehow brave, and somehow loyal, but he's actually just a traitor and a coward.

BONYEK: I said I was sorry.

PEEKA: No you didn't.

BONYEK: Well, I am.

PEEKA: Oh really?

BONYEK: Really.

PEEKA: I'm afraid we don't believe you, do we, Munib? The kind of person that would be sorry is the kind of person that wouldn't have done it in the first place.

BONYEK: It just kind of happened.

PEEKA: Yeah, and look what's 'just kind of happened' to us! (*Agitated scratching.*) Stuck here in pyjamas that itch like mad and smell like dogs in the rain! Every privilege gone! Munib's protoceratops a scrumpled up piece of paper! Fluffborough! My Fluffborough! Gone! Just a ball of nothingness in a hoover bag! The cathedral with its perfect spires! The bungalows for the elderly, the fountain in the park! The public toilet with its individual cubicles! The railway lines all plucked from Munib's head! Gone!

BONYEK: But you would have been in trouble anyway, even if I'd stayed!

PEEKA: Not as badly! Not if you'd said it was all your fault, like you promised! There may have been some loss of privileges, but not this! And anyway, that's not the point. The point is we trusted you and you turned out to be a pig. 'We vow to be loyal', that's the point.

BONYEK: I'm sorry, all right?

PEEKA: It's a bit late now.

BONYEK: Yeah, but /

PEEKA: The damage has been done.

BONYEK: I'm sorry!

PEEKA: So you keep saying.

BONYEK: What do you want me to say?

PEEKA: I'd rather you didn't say anything. I'd rather you kept your mouldy mouth shut until the year 2044.

(*Pause. PEEKA is overwhelmed by the itchiness of the pyjamas.*)

These stupid pyjamas, I could kill them!

(*PEEKA scratches and scratches. Pause.*)

BONYEK: You forgive me, don't you, Munib?

MUNIB: I don't think I can, I'm afraid.

PEEKA: See? Even Munib doesn't forgive you. And Munib forgives everything and everyone!

MUNIB: I would have stayed if your foot got stuck. You shouldn't make promises you're not brave enough to keep.

PEEKA: Well said.

BONYEK: But I'm keeping my promise. Look, I'm taking the punishment. And I'm sorry /

MUNIB: You're only sorry that you got caught, that doesn't count.

PEEKA: Well said again, Munib. That's two correct things you've said in a row.

MUNIB: And the worst thing is, you made us think we were going home. You made us believe The Mystery might get solved. You got our hopes up, that's the worst thing.

PEEKA: Well said again. To say three correct things in a row is excellent. Now, let's stop wasting time on this pathetic person and go to bed.

(*MUNIB and PEEKA climb onto their cold, naked beds.*)

BONYEK: If I'm so pathetic, how come it flew?

PEEKA: What flew?

BONYEK: Firework.

PEEKA: It didn't fly.

BONYEK: It lifted off the ground.

PEEKA: That thing? Fly? I've never heard anything more ridiculous!

BONYEK: Munib, tell her, it flew!

MUNIB: I don't know if it did or it didn't.

PEEKA: How could it? It's just three broken bikes and some sticks with feathers stuck on.

BONYEK: We pedalled too fast, that was the problem. Slow and steady's what it needs. (*Pause.*) You said, 'We're flying! We're flying!' It lifted off the ground, you know it did!

PEEKA: Fine, so it lifted off the ground! That's not flying! And anyway, do you really think that makes up for what you did to Royston? We know you drowned him. Always the same with you, isn't it, Bonyek? Letting people down in their hour of need. A false friend, that's what you are.

(*Scene ends with much restless scratching.*)

SCENE NINE

(*The ward. The middle of the night. MUNIB and PEEKA are asleep on their beds without sheets or pillows. BONYEK, his eyes still bandaged, is suffering a restless and tormented night of sleep. Distressed and delirious, he calls out...*)

BONYEK: Royston... Royston...!

(*The Ghost of ROYSTON appears on the ward, dripping wet from head to toe. BONYEK feels ROYSTON's presence.*)

Royston?

(*The restraining straps on Bed Number Four magically loosen and come away. BONYEK gets out of bed and starts searching for something on the floor.*)

I kept your shoe. I kept it...

(*He finds the shoe. He crawls across to ROYSTON and puts the shoe on ROYSTON's bare foot. ROYSTON pulls BONYEK up and holds him threateningly.*)

Please! It was an accident... I was trying to get a better grip!

(*ROYSTON rips the bandage from BONYEK's eyes and holds BONYEK's face up close to his own. BONYEK is frightened and elated to see his brother again.*)

Royston.

(*ROYSTON pushes BONYEK away. The key to the ward descends from above. BONYEK takes the key. BONYEK unlocks the door and goes. ROYSTON disappears. Scene ends.*)

SCENE TEN

(*Morning on the ward. PEEKA is asleep – twitching itchily on her cold, bare bed. MUNIB, who has just woken, feels his way to Bed Number Four. He runs his hands along the bed and finds it empty...*)

MUNIB: Bonyek? Bonyek?! Peeka, wake up!

PEEKA: (*Wakes up.*) What is it?

MUNIB: It's Bonyek, he's gone again.

PEEKA: What?!

MUNIB: I couldn't smell him. I came to check and he's gone.

PEEKA: Oh, grilliant.

MUNIB: He must have squirmed out bit by bit. I'll say one thing for our friend Bonyek, he's got guts.

PEEKA: No, Munib, guts are the opposite of what he's got. And a friend's the opposite of what he is. He's just a lying idiot who, once again, has dropped us in the cow pat!

MUNIB: Why are we in the cow pat?

PEEKA: For helping him escape. Nurse Cakebread will think we loosened his straps. And what did she say would happen if we did that?

MUNIB: Woebetide.

PEEKA: Exactly.

MUNIB: But I don't know what it means.

PEEKA: Neither do I, but I'm pretty sure it's worse than itchy pyjamas.

(*PEEKA tips the contents of The Barrel Of Oddments onto the floor. There is a draught excluder, a stringless ukelele, a few books, a rucksack, an umbrella, a cuddly puffin and a plant pot.*)

MUNIB: What are you doing?

PEEKA: We'll use the oddments to make a bulge in the bed. With any luck she'll see the bulge and not look any closer.

MUNIB: But…

PEEKA: (*Stuffing oddments into Bed Number Four.*) What?

MUNIB: Well, she'll see it's not him in the end. And then we'll be in even more trouble for being conniving.

PEEKA: Not necessarily. When she gets back from holiday she'll be tanned and relaxed and not so much in the mood for punishment. If we can just keep her fooled until she goes…

MUNIB: But…

PEEKA: What?

MUNIB: Well, what about the new Nurse Cakebread? How do we explain it to her?

PEEKA: We'll get rid of the bulge and tell her he's been sent to a different ward.

MUNIB: But Peeka…

PEEKA: What?!

MUNIB: I don't know. It just doesn't seem likely to work.

PEEKA: Have you got any better ideas?

MUNIB: No.

PEEKA: No?

MUNIB: No, but /

PEEKA: No! So stop criticising and be helpful!

(*MUNIB helps PEEKA in the making of the bogus BONYEK…*)

MUNIB: How did he escape, do you think? He was all strapped in and the door was locked.

PEEKA: How should I know? (*They are running out of oddments.*) What's going to look more like Bonyek's head, a cuddly puffin or the umbrella?

MUNIB: When I felt Bonyek's head in Habbagoogaloogaloo, it felt kind of telephone-shaped.

PEEKA: Telephone, good thinking!

(*PEEKA puts the cuddly puffin on the telephone ledge. She puts the telephone at the top of the bulge and covers the bulge with the sheet. It does not make for a very convincing BONYEK.*)

There. What do you think?

MUNIB: Perfect. But then I can't see anything.

(*NURSE CAKEBREAD enters in her going-on-holiday clothes. She has a tray of medicines. PEEKA and MUNIB stand by their beds and try to look innocent…*)

CAKEBREAD: Good morning, children. How did you all sleep?

PEEKA: Yes, Nurse Cakebread.

CAKEBREAD: Very good.

(PEEKA and MUNIB gulp down smallish cups of green medicine with nervous haste. NURSE CAKEBREAD approaches BONYEK's bed with a third cup of medicine in her hand. She seems certain to uncover the bogus BONYEK.)

Oh dear, is Bonyek worrying about his operation? Don't worry, Bonyek, I'm sure you'll be fine, dear.

(NURSE CAKEBREAD drinks the medicine herself. PEEKA and BONYEK breathe silent sighs of relief, but the danger is not over.)

I shall be off. I just thought you'd like to see me in my going-on-holiday clothes, Peeka.

PEEKA: They're lovely.

CAKEBREAD: Aren't they?

(NURSE CAKEBREAD eyes the bogus BONYEK quizzically.)

The next time you see me I shall be all tanned and relaxed.

PEEKA: Have a lovely time, Nurse Cakebread.

CAKEBREAD: In Zakynthos it's impossible not to have a lovely time. Aren't you pretty, Peeka?

PEEKA: Thank you, Nurse Cakebread.

(It seems that NURSE CAKEBREAD is about to leave – she has her hand on the door handle – but she turns back into the room…)

CAKEBREAD: Oh, and do behave for my sister-in-law, won't you?

MUNIB: Yes, Nurse Cakebread.

CAKEBREAD: I'm sure you will. You'll miss me, won't you?

PEEKA: Yes, Nurse Cakebread.

MUNIB: Yes, Nurse Cakebread.

CAKEBREAD: I'll miss you too.

(NURSE CAKEBREAD seems certain to leave the room – she is halfway out of the door. The telephone rings. The children wince. NURSE CAKEBREAD goes to where the telephone is normally kept and discovers the cuddly puffin. She inspects the cuddly puffin. Thinking that the cuddly puffin is ringing, she presses it to her ear. She sees the telephone cable leading to Bed Number Four…)

Once a Strangleman always a Strangleman.

(*She pulls back the sheet and answers the telephone…*)

Code Purple! Code! Purple!

(*The Code Purple siren begins to wail.*)

(*To both of them.*) After everything I've done. All the kindness I've shown…

(*NURSE CAKEBREAD is leaving the ward when the voice of SUPERINTENDENT RAINWATER comes through the speakers.*)

RAINWATER: Stay where you are, Nurse Cakebread.

CAKEBREAD: Superintendent Rainwater, this isn't my fault.

RAINWATER: Do not leave Children's Ward One.

CAKEBREAD: But the search…

RAINWATER: We'll leave the search to more effective members of staff. Also, I have no choice but to cancel your holiday.

CAKEBREAD: What?! But you can't, that was a reward from the Governors!

RAINWATER: And rewards are no longer appropriate. Just stay where you are, Nurse Cakebread.

(*SUPERINTENDENT RAINWATER is gone. NURSE CAKEBREAD is seething with anger. She picks up the receiver of the phone and dials a single number.*)

CAKEBREAD: Joyce. Have the Emergency Generator sent over. Don't ask questions. (*She replaces the receiver.*) If Nurse Cakebread can't go to Zakynthos, Zakynthos will just have to come to Nurse Cakebread.

(*Scene ends.*)

SCENE ELEVEN

(*The ward, a few minutes later. A massive machine has been brought in – The Original Generator. It takes the form of a two-berth treadmill with various dials, flashing lights and screens attached to it. A copper rod, about two metres in length, sticks out of the side of The Original Generator. Dangling from the end of the copper rod is a gigantic red heating lamp. MUNIB and PEEKA look nervously at the ominous machine…*)

CAKEBREAD: This is The Original Generator. Who can tell me what a generator is?

MUNIB: A thing that generates things?

CAKEBREAD: That's correct, Akmed.

MUNIB: My name's Munib.

CAKEBREAD: I'll call you whatever I like! (*Pause.*) History lesson. When St Ruth's was first built, there was a prison next door. This gave the first Governor of St Ruth's a 'grilliant' idea. Why spend money on heating when free energy could be generated by the prisoners? And so, five generators were built, and the prisoners came in shifts to work the treadmills and bring warmth to our patients. Well, sadly, the second Governor was a rather pathetic man called Jeremy Ankle-Bandage who had the generators scrapped. All except this one, which was kept for use in the most extreme circumstances.

(*NURSE CAKEBREAD slips off her clothes to reveal a hideous bathing costume.*)

I'd call this an extreme circumstance, wouldn't you? Onto the treadmill.

(*PEEKA leads MUNIB to the treadmill. NURSE CAKEBREAD wheels a bed to a position beneath the heating lamp. She slots the umbrella into the bed – like the window opening pole in Scene One – to create a parasol. She reclines on the bed.*)

I think a bit of relaxation in hot conditions is the very least Nurse Cakebread deserves, don't you?

MUNIB: Yes, Nurse Cakebread.

CAKEBREAD: Come on, then, what are you waiting for?!

(*PEEKA and MUNIB start to walk on the treadmill. As they walk the heating lamp begins to glow.*)

The average temperature in Zakynthos is thirty-eight degrees celsius. That's really very hot.

PEEKA: Yes, Nurse Cakebread.

CAKEBREAD: A little faster then, please.

(*They speed up a bit. NURSE CAKEBREAD takes out a book and reads from it...*)

'A Violet Nosegay by Mariella Haberdash. Chapter One, The Arrival Of The Handsome Vicar.'

(*She reads. The children toil.*)

MUNIB: Peeka.

PEEKA: What?

MUNIB: Do we have to do this for the rest of our lives?

PEEKA: Possibly.

CAKEBREAD: No chatter.

(*She reads. The children toil.*)

MUNIB: Peeka.

PEEKA: What?

MUNIB: What happens when we need the toilet?

CAKEBREAD: Quiet! (*Pause.*) A little faster, please. Nurse Cakebread would like to feel as if she were being roasted.

(*They speed up. The children are beginning to struggle. NURSE CAKEBREAD reads aloud from 'A Violet Nosegay'.*)

'The new vicar swept the sandy-coloured hair from his face and looked deep into Olivia's brown-coloured eyes.'

MUNIB: Nurse Cakebread...

CAKEBREAD: '"Hello," said Olivia who smelt of tulips.'

MUNIB: Nurse Cakebread...

CAKEBREAD: '"Hello," said the new vicar, with a face that was becoming nearly purple-coloured. "I'm the new vicar."'

MUNIB: Nurse Cakebread...

CAKEBREAD: What?!

MUNIB: (*Fighting for breath.*) Nurse Cakebread... Please... I can't... When do we get to stop?

(*NURSE CAKEBREAD calmly puts her book down and approaches The Original Generator.*)

CAKEBREAD: I'll tell you when you get to stop. When you're truly sorry for your part in spoiling Nurse Cakebread's holiday plans, that's when you get to stop.

MUNIB: But we are sorry /

(*NURSE CAKEBREAD begins to lose control. She grabs the window-opening pole and smacks the Emergency Generator as she speaks…*)

CAKEBREAD: When the words kindness, obedience and respect actually mean something to you. When you've shown me the loyalty I deserve. When the sweat runs down my body in great rivers, as it does in Zakynthos, that's when, and not before! And not before!

BONYEK: (*Off.*) Leave them alone!!!

CAKEBREAD: Who said that?!

BONYEK: (*Off.*) I did!!!

(*PEEKA and MUNIB stop walking and NURSE CAKEBREAD turns to see BONYEK enter the ward. He has covered his clothes in feathers.*)

I, Bonyek Lesley Strangleman! Brother to a dead hero, friend to these good people, here to bring justice to them all! And unless you want a face full of feathers, I suggest you listen to me! (*Threatens her with feathers.*)

CAKEBREAD: (*Cowers.*) Get away. Get away!

PEEKA: Where did you get the feathers?

BONYEK: From Firework, she's still outside. Don't much like feathers, do you, Cakebread?

CAKEBREAD: How do you know that?

BONYEK: Well! I first got suspicious when I had that feather in my hair last night. Then I saw feathers listed as a 'dislike' on your page of the hospital website. But it was only when I saw 'Nurse Cakebread Hates Feathers' on the wall of the boys' toilet that I knew I'd found your weakness. Come down, you two.

(*PEEKA and MUNIB come down from The Original Generator.*)

CAKEBREAD: It's a bit late, Bonyek, don't you think? To be playing the hero. We know he's not a hero, don't we, children? He's a coward. A coward and a drowner!

BONYEK: Well, let's just see about that. (*He holds up a piece of paper.*) In my hand I hold freedom from rubbish!

MUNIB: What do you mean?

CAKEBREAD: Where did you get that?

BONYEK: I saw it on your desk yesterday. I thought it looked fishy, so I snuck back and nabbed it in the night.

MUNIB: (*Sniffs the air.*) Peeka, it's from your mum.

BONYEK: (*Gives PEEKA the letter.*) Read it out.

PEEKA: 'Dear Nurse Cakebread, I'm so sad that there has been complications with Peeka's operation, and it's not safe to visit. Please give her this box of gooey-centred chocolates' /

BONYEK: (*To CAKEBREAD.*) Empty that bikini pocket!

(*NURSE CAKEBREAD reluctantly empties a pocket in her bikini. It is full of shiny chocolate wrappers.*)

Well looky look, wrappers off gooey-centred chocolates. Carry on.

PEEKA: '…and tell her that I love her, and tell us when it's safe to visit.'

BONYEK: (*He waves another letter.*) And another from Munib's mum, just the same. But the operations were successful. (*He waves a third document.*) It says so here, signed by the Visiting Surgeon! The only reason they've not been visiting is cos you said they couldn't.

MUNIB: The Mystery… Solved…!

BONYEK: (*To PEEKA and MUNIB.*) You should have gone home months ago.

PEEKA: But…why?

BONYEK: Yeah, why did you do it, Cakebread? Surely not just for the chocs.

CAKEBREAD: (*To PEEKA and MUNIB.*) Because you like it here with me. You're happy here. We're a family. We are, we're a family.

(*No answer.*)

BONYEK: There's a phone number on the top of that letter, Cakebread. Why don't you ring it?

(*NURSE CAKEBREAD takes the letter and dials a number from it.*)

CAKEBREAD: Mrs Siddiqi? Munib's made a full recovery. You can collect him right away.

(*Scene ends.*)

SCENE TWELVE

(*BONYEK watches as PEEKA and MUNIB remove their bandages. NURSE CAKEBREAD watches from a distance. MUNIB is delighted by the first rush of light and colour to his brain in many weeks. PEEKA and MUNIB hug BONYEK. NURSE CAKEBREAD takes BONYEK away for his operation. He goes out and NURSE CAKEBREAD follows.*)

SCENE THIRTEEN

(*MUNIB and PEEKA are almost ready to leave. They wear coats over their pyjamas. They look around at the place that has been their home for so long.*)

MUNIB: It's funny. I'm almost kind of scared to leave.

PEEKA: Me too.

(*Pause.*)

MUNIB: He'll be having his operation right now I reckon.

PEEKA: He's lucky he got a morning appointment. The surgeon doesn't shake so much in the mornings.

(*Pause.*)

MUNIB: It doesn't feel right, just leaving him. Specially now Cakebread wants to kill him and stuff.

PEEKA: Maybe he'll escape again.

MUNIB: How? There's only one way out and security's on double high alert.

PEEKA: I suppose. (*Pause.*) Although…

MUNIB: What?

PEEKA: Maybe there's another way out.

MUNIB: (*Looks around.*) Where?

PEEKA: (*Points up.*) If we timed it right…

PEEKA: He did say Firework's still there.

MUNIB: Peeka, that's a grilliant idea! Let's leave him a note. (*He produces a pen and paper.*) You write, my eyes are still blurry. Write 'We will fly in on Firework and rescue you during the Minute Of Air!'

PEEKA: (*Writes.*) 'We will fly in on Firework and rescue you during the Minute Of Air!'

(*She puts the note in BONYEK's bed. Pause.*)

PEEKA: How though?

MUNIB: What do you mean?

PEEKA: We could hardly get her off the ground with all three of us. With just us two we don't stand a chance. And for all we know, they might have taken Firework away. It's never going to work.

(*They are despondent. NURSE CAKEBREAD enters.*)

CAKEBREAD: Children, your parents are waiting at reception.

PEEKA: Goodbye, Nurse Cakebread.

MUNIB: Goodbye, Nurse Cakebread.

CAKEBREAD: Yes, goodbye, children. If you're ever passing by do pop in and say hello to dear old Nurse Cake /

(*MUNIB slams the door behind him, leaving NURSE CAKEBREAD alone in the room. Scene ends.*)

SCENE FOURTEEN

(*BONYEK is asleep in his bed, recovering from his operation. One of his eyes is bandaged. He wakes up. He is uncomfortable – he can feel a scrumpled up piece of paper pressing against his skin. Still groggy, he reads what is written on the piece of paper...)*

BONYEK: 'We will fly in on Firework and rescue you during the Minute Of Air!'

(*BONYEK grins and hides the note as NURSE CAKEBREAD enters.*)

CAKEBREAD: How are you feeling? Has the anaesthetic worn off? (*He ignores her.*) I think Bonyek Strangleman thinks he's taught Nurse Cakebread a lesson. In fairness. What Bonyek doesn't realise is Nurse Cakebread has no lessons to learn in that area. She's very fair, as you will see over the coming months.

(*NURSE CAKEBREAD produces a little mallet.*)

Sit up, I need to test your reactions.

(*She whacks his knee with the mallet.*)

Good.

(*She whacks it harder.*)

Excellent. Can you feel this?

(*She pinches his nipple.*)

BONYEK: Yeah.

CAKEBREAD: And what about when I twist?

(*He winces and nods.*)

Good.

(*She sets about triple-locking the door, cutting off the phone etc...*)

I telephoned your home. Nobody's planning to visit you. Oh, and I spoke to Munib and Peeka's parents too. Explained our little misunderstanding with the letters.

BONYEK: Nurse Cakebread.

CAKEBREAD: Yes, Bonyek?

BONYEK: What time is it?

CAKEBREAD: Twenty to three.

BONYEK: Do you want me to go on The Original Generator? Cos it must be well hot in Zakynthos this time of day. And it's my fault more than anyone's you ain't there now.

(*She studies BONYEK suspiciously.*)

CAKEBREAD: Very well.

(*BONYEK gets out of bed and onto The Original Generator. NURSE CAKEBREAD reclines as before. BONYEK begins to pedal.*)

BONYEK: How's that then?

CAKEBREAD: Yes, that's rather good, Bonyek. For someone that just woke up from surgery. A little warmer though, please.

(*BONYEK speeds up.*)

BONYEK: So, it's nice in Zakynthos, is it?

CAKEBREAD: Nice? It's a paradise. (*Growing sleepy.*) A sleepy sunkissed paradise.

BONYEK: I bet it's well nice. With the sun roasting down on your skin all day till you're warm as toast.

CAKEBREAD: Such glorious sunshine…

(*As with the dolphin-feeding expedition and the early morning battle, the environment begins to change…*)

BONYEK: And the taste of pineapply drinks all tingling in your mouth. And the blueness of the sky. And the jangly foreign music in the background. And hands rubbing sun cream up your neck and shoulders.

CAKEBREAD: (*Wriggles with delight.*) Mmmmm…

BONYEK: And the waves gliding over the sand in a rhythm like a lovely whisper.

(*BONYEK climbs down from the machine and the heating lamp no longer glows. He fills a bucket with quick-drying cement…*)

CAKEBREAD: Why is it getting colder?

BONYEK: That's just the breeze coming in off the sea, cooling the blood, and bringing smells of octopus and lobsters and fish you can have for your tea.

(*BONYEK sticks NURSE CAKEBREAD's feet in the bucket of quick-drying cement...*)

Can you feel the lovely sand between your toes?

CAKEBREAD: Do you know, I really can.

BONYEK: And if you listen, you can even hear the waves, Nurse Cakebread...

(*BONYEK turns on the sprinklers...*)

CAKEBREAD: They don't...sound like waves...

BONYEK: Oh, but they are! Big, beautiful, majestic waves, keeping you cool with their lovely spray. Can you feel it, Nurse Cakebread?

(*He flicks water on NURSE CAKEBREAD.*)

CAKEBREAD: Yes, I can feel it... I can feel it...!

BONYEK: Go to sleep now, Nurse Cakebread. Everything's going to be just lovely.

(*The water level is rising. Scene ends.*)

SCENE FIFTEEN

(*A few moments later. The water in the ward is now three feet deep. NURSE CAKEBREAD wakes, her hair already wet. She sits up and spits out a mouthful of water. She looks around her and screams.*)

BONYEK: Hello, Nurse Cakebread, how are you?

CAKEBREAD: Bonyek...?

BONYEK: Nice little sleep?

CAKEBREAD: What have you done?

BONYEK: Oh, you mean all the water?

CAKEBREAD: Yes, the water!

BONYEK: I turned on the sprinklers.

CAKEBREAD: Well turn them off!

BONYEK: Thought the old place could do with a rinse.

CAKEBREAD: Turn them off! Now!

BONYEK: No, I reckon I'll give the place a good clean.

(*NURSE CAKEBREAD gets to her feet but finds she can't walk.*)

CAKEBREAD: My feet!

BONYEK: What's that?

CAKEBREAD: My feet, what have you done to them?!

BONYEK: Oh yeah, had a bit of an accident with some quick-drying cement. Sorry about that.

CAKEBREAD: Please! Turn them off now or we'll both drown.

BONYEK: You might but I won't!

CAKEBREAD: Of course you'll drown! You're not a fish!

BONYEK: I'm going to get rescued.

CAKEBREAD: Rescued?! Nobody's going to rescue you!

BONYEK: What time do you make it, Cakebread?

(*NURSE CAKEBREAD looks at her watch. The water has risen to the level of her chest and she is panicking.*)

CAKEBREAD: Three o'clock...

BONYEK: That's right, three o'clock!

(*A loud buzz marks the beginning of The Minute Of Air. The roof retracts and the ward fills with sunshine and birdsong. The Flying Machine is nowhere to be seen.*)

Where are they?!

CAKEBREAD: What?

BONYEK: Munib?! Peeka?! No!!

CAKEBREAD: Bonyek, you didn't think...? (*She laughs wildly.*) You silly boy, they don't care about you! And that thing was never going to fly!

BONYEK: Oh, wasn't it?!

(*The Flying Machine, with PEEKA and MUNIB pedalling, rowing and somehow steering, begins its descent into the ward. They wear swimming goggles and speak through cardboard megaphones.*)

MUNIB: Stand back. Firework descending. Stand back. Firework descending.

BONYEK: Flip me, you did it!

PEEKA: Slow and steady and she flies like a dream.

BONYEK: Grilliant!

(*BONYEK climbs onto the flying machine.*)

CAKEBREAD: But what about me?

BONYEK: What about you, Cakebread?

CAKEBREAD: You can't leave me to drown!

BONYEK: I thought that's what I was! A drowner!

PEEKA: Give us one good reason why not!

CAKEBREAD: I…don't have any.

MUNIB: Then beg!

CAKEBREAD: Please!

BONYEK: Not very nice, is it, Cakebread?

MUNIB: To be made to feel tiny and weak!

PEEKA: To have someone else make up all the rules!

MUNIB: To be forced to beg!

(*NURSE CAKEBREAD is beginning to drown. BONYEK turns off the sprinklers and pulls out the plug.*)

BONYEK: We hope you've learnt your lesson, Nurse Cakebread! We hope you've learnt your lesson!

(*As The Flying Machine flies up through the roof and the roof returns to normal, the water drains away. The plughole lets out an almighty gurgle.*

NURSE CAKEBREAD stands in her bucket of cement, a pathetic, bedraggled and tiny figure. She starts moving towards the door – perhaps shuffling in her bucket, perhaps rolling in a lying down position…)

RAINWATER: (*Relayed through a speaker.*) Nurse Cakebread, this is Superintendent Rainwater. Report to my office immediately. It is understood you've been misusing The Original Generator. Report to my office immediately. Can you hear me Nurse Cakebread?

CAKEBREAD: Yes, Kimberley, I can hear you! And I'm not coming. I'm going home. I'm going home and I'm never coming back.

(*NURSE CAKEBREAD finally reaches the door and leaves.*)

RAINWATER: Nurse Cakebread? Nurse Cakebread? Nurse Cakebread!

(*Scene ends.*)

SCENE SIXTEEN

(*ROYSTON's ghost stands alone. BONYEK approaches nervously. They look at one another. ROYSTON opens his arms to BONYEK in forgiveness and they hug. Scene ends. Play Ends.*)

SMASHED EGGS

Characters

ANGELA

MIRANDA

TITUS

THE MOUTH COLLECTOR

Smashed Eggs was first produced at the Arena Theatre in Wolverhampton on 5 February 2002, in a production by Pentabus Theatre, with the following cast:

MIRANDA, Beverley Denim

TITUS, Darren Cheek

ANGELA, Nia Davies

Director Dani Parr

Designer Kate Bunce

ACT ONE

(*All of Act One takes place in ANGELA's house. Like other houses it has beds, tables, chairs, kitchen stuff and other things. Unlike other houses its walls, ornaments and furniture are meticulously decorated to display in writing one or more of the house rules. There are many house rules.*

The stage is in darkness. A tape recording of ANGELA speaking plays on a tape machine.)

ANGELA: No putting beer into anybody's ear. No climbing into the refrigerator. Be careful with the ornaments…

(*A very slight light picks out TITUS and MIRANDA, asleep in their beds.*)

All underwear must be green. No setting fire to things. No sunbathing underneath tennis rackets…

(*Alarm clocks buzz in strange stereo.*)

Never scratch your nose in the month of December…

(*The children silence the alarms and the tapes.*)

MIRANDA: Open your eyes, cabbage head.

TITUS: They're already open, cow head.

(*MIRANDA turns a light on.*)

MIRANDA: Oh yes, there they are, peeping out from the ugliest face in the world.

TITUS: Try looking in the mirror, then you'll see a really ugly face.

(*MIRANDA and TITUS tidy their beds away. As they speak they dress…*)

I wish you wouldn't make this room so hot.

MIRANDA: You're the one producing all the hot gas.

TITUS: My brain is like an actual volcano.

MIRANDA: My brain is twice as hot as yours.

TITUS: No way.

MIRANDA: Any day. Come to think of it, my head is probably this hot because I just had the most amazing dream in the history of sleep.

TITUS: Only one dream? I had six thousand.

MIRANDA: Get lost you never.

TITUS: I did. First I dreamt I was a seahorse, then I dreamt I was an eagle, then I dreamt I was a tiger in a palace in a jungle.

MIRANDA: If you were a tiger they'd kick you out of the jungle.

TITUS: Actually, I ate the lion and curled up on his throne.

MIRANDA: You'd be kicked out by a group of mice for being such a coward. And anyway, I think a tiger would know which shoe to put on which foot.

(*TITUS looks at his feet and sees his mistake.*)

TITUS: Tigers don't wear shoes. Ignoramus.

MIRANDA: Anyway, mine was a nightmare, so you can shut up.

TITUS: Every dream's a nightmare for a weakling girl like you.

MIRANDA: Listen who's talking, Mummy's little treasure. It was about a man called The Mouth Collector.

TITUS: Watch me wet my pants.

MIRANDA: Who hasn't got a mouth on his face.

(*TITUS shrugs a bit nervously. MIRANDA continues, creeping towards TITUS with arms outstretched in a genuinely menacing way.*)

He spends the night-time roaming round and stealing other people's mouths. You can try to run away, but he just keeps catching up. And the white bits in his eyes are red. And his hands are strong as eagle claws. And his home feels like a spider's web. If you ever went there, he'd pick your squashy little mouth off your squashy little face like a magnet off a fridge.

TITUS: Have you finished? Thank goodness for that, I nearly died of boredom.

MIRANDA: You'll die of something else if you don't check on the Animal and wake your mummy up.

TITUS: Brush your hair. It looks like a dirty bird's nest.

(*TITUS leaves, tripping on something as he goes. MIRANDA begins to brush the knots from her hair. TITUS goes to where ANGELA sleeps. He picks up her slippers, brushes the fluff from them and places them on the floor. Beside her bed is a gong. He strikes it gently and speaks slightly wearily…*)

Wake up. It's seven o'clock and all the birds are chirping.

(*ANGELA does not wake. TITUS stands on one leg and strikes the gong again.*)

Wake up. It's seven o'clock and the owls and the hedgehogs are drifting off to sleep.

ANGELA: Is that my little baby kangaroo?

TITUS: Please don't call me baby kangaroo.

ANGELA: Have you brushed the fluff from my slippers?

TITUS: There was no fluff, but I brushed them anyway.

ANGELA: Is my dressing gown in the warm cupboard?

TITUS: You saw me put it there last night.

ANGELA: And have you checked on the Animal's health?

TITUS: Yeah. Still bad. He didn't even squeak when I poked him with the celery.

(*ANGELA sits up in bed.*)

ANGELA: Poor old Animal. He seems to get weaker every day.

TITUS: Dear old Animal.

ANGELA: Illness is a terrible thing. He wouldn't survive ten minutes without his special cage and diet. Poor old Animal.

TITUS: Dear old Animal.

(*TITUS fetches the dressing gown from the warm cupboard.*)

Is Miranda awake?

TITUS: Awake and behaving like she owns the world.

ANGELA: Titus –

TITUS: Awake and spouting on as if no-one else existed.

ANGELA: I'm sure she's only trying to be friendly.

TITUS: That girl is such an irritating stomach-ache.

ANGELA: Why do you say that?

TITUS: One, she draws pictures of me when I'm asleep. Two, she picks up earwigs and says they look like me. Three, she hides my toothbrush and five, she says that I've got nappy rash. And I never do anything to her.

ANGELA: I thought you two were friends.

TITUS: Friends do not put spiders in each other's shoes.

(*TITUS puts ANGELA's slippers on.*)

Why can't she live somewhere else? I preferred it when it was just you, me and Animal.

ANGELA: You know that's not possible.

TITUS: She's a pain in the absolute neck.

ANGELA: Well, I suppose there might be a bit of room for one or two new rules. We'll make an earwig rule. And we'll make a spider rule. And we'll make a very special rule about not drawing people when they're asleep.

TITUS: What about my toothbrush?

ANGELA: I must have told you what happens to people who hide toothbrushes. If they do it one too many times, their teeth go yellow and their ears go flaky.

TITUS: That would serve her completely right.

ANGELA: Be patient with her, Titus. Try to see things through her eyes. She has been through a terrible amount.

TITUS: That doesn't mean she can –

ANGELA: You like her really.

TITUS: I'll try not to get too annoyed with her stupid behaviour.

ANGELA: I think we should get breakfast on the boil, don't you?

(*ANGELA and TITUS enter the breakfast area. MIRANDA is sitting at the table. It is laid with three plates and three large plastic spoons. There is an egg-holding ornament positioned quite prominently which holds three eggs. ANGELA looks out of the window.*)

TITUS: Good morning, Miranda. You look well.

MIRANDA: Really? You look like a bag of dead worms.

ANGELA: Rain is definitely on the way.

MIRANDA: I cooked the breakfast, Angela. It's all in that whacking great saucepan. I had to do something while you two were chatting.

ANGELA: Thank you, Miranda.

MIRANDA: And before you ask, I followed all the rules for cooking breakfast. All forty-six of them.

(*ANGELA begins to spoon peas onto the plates. One spoonful for herself and two for each of the children.*)

ANGELA: A hundred peas for Titus. A hundred peas for Miranda. And fifty peas for me.

TITUS: Peas remind me of planets.

MIRANDA: Peas remind me of your brain. Green, squashy and not very big.

ANGELA: What a glorious smell.

MIRANDA: It's a shame they taste like balls of mud.

(*Pause.*)

Why do we always eat peas for breakfast?

ANGELA: Because it's a rule. It's painted on the wall.

MIRANDA: Only because you painted it there. No-one else in the world eats peas for breakfast.

ANGELA: And they suffer the consequences. These peas are why your brains stay round and firm, while the brains of other children turn soft like eggs or dry like toast or sticky like Marmite.

TITUS: Or gloopy like porridge.

MIRANDA: We could at least have fish then. What about kippers?

TITUS: Anyone that eats fish for breakfast grows claws like a crab or a lobster. Sorry, we thought everyone knew that.

ANGELA: Perhaps tomorrow we'll have a change. Treat ourselves by putting in a sprig of mint. But that's enough ungrateful talk for now.

(*Simultaneously, each drops two sugar cubes into their cup of tea and stirs with a teaspoon. ANGELA holds her spoon aloft.*)

Rules for breakfast please.

TITUS: Breakfast must be eaten with a large plastic spoon.

MIRANDA: Breakfast must consist of peas and only peas.

TITUS: No making up songs about breakfast.

MIRANDA: No pretending your peas are an army.

TITUS: No pushing peas about your plate…

MIRANDA: … Or putting them in pictures, patterns or lines.

TITUS: No speaking on behalf of peas.

MIRANDA: No banging of plastic spoons.

TITUS: No spilling.

MIRANDA: No yawning.

TITUS: No salt without pepper.

MIRANDA: No swallowing without chewing.

TITUS: No flicking.

(*TITUS puts salt on his peas and MIRANDA does the same with pepper and ANGELA with vinegar. They speak all at once…*)

TITUS: Salt!

MIRANDA: Pepper!

ANGELA: Vinegar!

(*They slickly switch condiments and do the same thing.*)

TITUS: Pepper!

MIRANDA: Vinegar!

ANGELA: Salt!

(*And again.*)

TITUS: Vinegar!

MIRANDA: Salt!

ANGELA: Pepper!

(*ANGELA and TITUS rest their little fingers on their noses. Forgetting the next part of the ritual, MIRANDA is about to eat a spoonful of peas.*)

Hold your horses, eager beaver.

(*MIRANDA puts her fingers on her nose.*)

Thank you for the healthy plate of peas I'm about to eat.

TITUS: For dolphinariums, planetariums, ankles and feet.

MIRANDA: For crumpets and for trumpets and for sheep that bleat.

ANGELA: Thank you for the healthy plate of peas I am about to eat. Thank you for this appetising meal.

TITUS: For mixing bowls and telegraph poles and the invention of the wheel.

MIRANDA: For oranges and oranges and bits of orange peel.

ANGELA: But most of all, thank you for this appetising meal.

(*MIRANDA and TITUS set about eating their peas with their plastic spoons. They take mouthfuls simultaneously. ANGELA cannot see how much they hate the peas.*)

There's nothing I like better than to see a child enjoying a plateful of peas.

TITUS: They are delicious.

ANGELA: And how lucky we are to have lovely fresh peas, picked from our pretty pea patch, grown in well-drained soil and enriched with well-rotted farmyard manure.

(*MIRANDA spits out some peas.*)

MIRANDA: Cow's muck?!

TITUS: It's all part of the fertilisation process.

ANGELA: They're perfectly clean.

TITUS: Peas are rich in protein, vitamins, dietary fibre and mineral salts.

ANGELA: That's absolutely correct.

MIRANDA: It's a shame they taste like curled-up woodlice.

(*MIRANDA resumes eating.*)

ANGELA: A lot of work goes into the growing of these peas. Digging, watering, picking and protecting them from danger. Protecting them from the cold and from mice and pea moths and bean weevils. Look at you both. Like a pair of perfect peas in a pod. And it's my job to protect you from the dangers of –

TITUS: Miranda!

MIRANDA: What?

TITUS: She's pretending her peas are an army!

MIRANDA: Titus!

TITUS: Look at that!

MIRANDA: I hate you for saying that!

ANGELA: Let me see.

TITUS: It's as plain as the nose on her face! The big pea is obviously the Sergeant Major and the ones in a line are his regiment! And look! She's even using the pepper as a gunpowder store!

ANGELA: This is extremely serious.

MIRANDA: I don't know what anyone's going on about.

(*MIRANDA scrambles the peas up.*)

TITUS: She's scrambled them up now!

MIRANDA: It was a coincidence, pig face!

ANGELA: I sincerely hope that's true, Miranda. I have told you many times what happens to people pretending their peas are an army. They're sent away to fight in wars, okay Miranda? Unfamiliar countries and dangerous situations. So don't come crying to me if the Prime Minister knocks on our door –

MIRANDA: It wasn't on purpose.

ANGELA: I sincerely hope that's true.

MIRANDA: They got in a line by themselves.

ANGELA: War is not to be trifled with.

TITUS: I'd miss you terribly –

MIRANDA: Shut up, baby. I'll get you for that.

(*Silence but for the munching of peas.*)

Angela... I know that a rule is a rule is a rule. But why are people that pretend their peas are an army sent away to fight in wars?

ANGELA: There's no point in questioning what happens to be.

MIRANDA: But some of it doesn't make sense.

TITUS: Perhaps your brain just isn't ready –

MIRANDA: Like why do people that try to see into the future grow holly bushes in their heads? Where does the holly even come from? Or why do people that sniff too much go blind? Or why would peanuts make me sick?

ANGELA: You're allergic to peanuts.

TITUS: You are allergic to peanuts.

MIRANDA: Okay, I'm allergic but... There's too many rules when all I want to do is muck about. I feel like I'm drowning in a box –

TITUS: Somebody climbed out of bed the wrong side.

MIRANDA: Before I moved here I was always –

ANGELA: We mustn't upset ourselves with thinking about the past. I set the rules to make you safe. And to help you to be happy. And because I love you both so much. You understand that, don't you?

(*ANGELA affectionately puts her hand on MIRANDA's shoulder. MIRANDA freezes. ANGELA takes it away again.*)

MIRANDA: I didn't mean to arrange my peas like that.

ANGELA: I'll phone the Prime Minister later on and tell him that it was a false alarm. Now, if we're all finished, I think it's probably time we fed the Animal.

(*TITUS, MIRANDA and ANGELA move to the Animal's cage. Ceremoniously, TITUS lifts a sheet from the cage to reveal Animal: a mangy and startled but lovable creature. They peer at him gloomily.*)

MIRANDA: Is he still breathing?

TITUS: Only very slightly. Poor old sick old Animal.

ANGELA: Dear old poor old Animal. I don't suppose you've got much appetite.

(ANGELA drops a biscuit into the cage.)

TITUS: His teeth are getting blunter and his eyes are all tired and blank. They look a bit like tiny scratched black marbles.

(TITUS drops a carrot into the cage.)

MIRANDA: Look, there's a scab on his back in the shape of a violin. And his legs are getting thinner.

(MIRANDA drops a worm into the cage.)

ANGELA: Your fur used to be so soft to stroke.

MIRANDA: What's the actual matter with him, Angela?

ANGELA: Illness, I'm afraid. A combination of germs and viruses is gumming up his poor little blood. Terrible horrible animal illness. Without the rules I set him and without his special diet he'd have passed away a week or two ago.

(They sigh.)

TITUS: May I have permission to go and do my painting? I want to paint the stripes on the tiger's face.

ANGELA: Good boy.

(MIRANDA pulls a face at TITUS as he leaves. Pause.)

MIRANDA: May I have permission to…go and brush my hair again? It gets all knotted up and stuff dead quickly.

ANGELA: Sit down for a minute.

MIRANDA: Please Angela, I can feel it knotting up.

ANGELA: Sit down and chat to me for a while.

(MIRANDA sits down on a chair. ANGELA kneels close in front of her and inspects her face, making MIRANDA uncomfortable.)

MIRANDA: It might rain later –

ANGELA: I'm worried about your general well-being, Miranda. I'm worried that your general feelings might not be too cheerful.

MIRANDA: I don't know what you mean.

ANGELA: Your head is like a clenched fist.

MIRANDA: I don't know what you mean.

ANGELA: It's perfectly natural. You've been through a terrible amount. With all that sadness and settling in here, it's perfectly understandable if you feel…a little anxious day to day.

MIRANDA: I don't feel a little anxious day to day.

ANGELA: Then that's good. But I hope you know that if you ever do feel at all anxious or frightened or peculiar, I hope you know how much I'd like to help.

(*MIRANDA nods. Satisfied, ANGELA stands up and sets about writing or painting something on the side of the washing-up bowl.*)

MIRANDA: I had a dream last night.

ANGELA: Oh really? Tell me about your dream.

MIRANDA: It was about a man called The Mouth Collector.

ANGELA: What a funny imagination.

MIRANDA: Yeah. Only it wasn't funny, it was horrible. He really loved his wife and baby, but they disappeared. Then a while after that, his mouth disappeared as well. So… In the daytime, he hides in his special secret home with this nasty long-eared rabbit and his other special things. Then at night, he creeps around the world and steals other people's mouths. He picks them off our faces like apples off a tree. And The Mouth Collector's hands are strong and his eyes are red and his arms are twisted and he wears this special secret mask, Angela. And the mask is like… And all the secret things, they look all… I don't remember what they look like but the whole thing was just so creepy. I woke up and my head was like a boiling kettle.

ANGELA: Perhaps you're getting sick.

MIRANDA: I was so scared, I could hardly breathe.

(*ANGELA puts her hand on MIRANDA's forehead.*)

I could hardly move.

ANGELA: My goodness, you are burning up. And look at the shopping bags under your eyes.

MIRANDA: I don't need medicine if that's what you're driving at.

ANGELA: Let's see…

(*MIRANDA follows the following instructions…*)

Stand up. Stick out your tongue. Close your eyes. Clap. Stick out your bottom. Put your fingers in your ears. Jump up and down on the spot.

(*MIRANDA does not jump up and down as she cannot hear this instruction. ANGELA takes MIRANDA's fingers from her ears.*)

It doesn't seem to be anything too serious. Perhaps I'll fetch you some medicine all the same.

MIRANDA: No, please –

ANGELA: It's better to be safe than it is to be sorry.

MIRANDA: Please Angela, don't make me drink that stuff.

ANGELA: Titus! Come here my little baby kangaroo!

(*TITUS enters immediately wearing a beret and holding a palette and a paintbrush.*)

TITUS: Please don't call me 'baby kangaroo'. It makes me sound like a baby kangaroo.

ANGELA: Miranda needs some medicine so I'm going to the chemist. While I'm gone, it being Saturday, I'd like you two to mop the floor. Okay?

(*ANGELA gives out mops.*)

A mop for Titus. And a mop for Miranda. I don't want squabbles or anyone skiving. Just working together nicely, is that clear?

TITUS / MIRANDA: Yes.

ANGELA: Good.

(*ANGELA holds a hand aloft. TITUS and MIRANDA put on mackintoshes as they recite…*)

Rules for mopping please.

TITUS: No pretending your mop is a snooker cue.

MIRANDA: Mackintoshes must be worn.

TITUS: No pretending your mop is a microphone.

MIRANDA: No shoving mops into other people's faces.

TITUS: One scoop of soap per bucket.

MIRANDA: One mop per person.

TITUS: No scrapping or skidding…

MIRANDA: … Or pretend sword-fighting with mops.

ANGELA: Good. I should just make it there and back before it
starts to rain. Can I trust you both to behave?

(*MIRANDA puts her arm around TITUS.*)

MIRANDA: Us two? We'll be as good as gold, won't we old
buddy?

TITUS: I'll make sure she doesn't do anything stupid.

(*MIRANDA stamps on TITUS' foot. It hurts.*)

MIRANDA: Was that your foot? Sorry old chum.

ANGELA: And try to get Animal to eat something while I'm
away. His poor little body's getting so thin and weak.

MIRANDA: No problem. Leave everything in our capable
hands.

ANGELA: Must change out of these pyjamas.

(*ANGELA exits. The children part immediately and MIRANDA
starts mopping the arm that was round TITUS' shoulder.*)

You are such a creepy little whining little bootlicker, Titus.
You're always trying to get me into trouble.

TITUS: It's not my fault if you can't control yourself.

MIRANDA: I wasn't even pretending that my peas were an
army. I was pretending my peas were a pop concert.

TITUS: I'm not an idiot, you know.

MIRANDA: You could have fooled me in that idiot-brained hat.

TITUS: There's no need to be personal.

(*TITUS takes the hat off and strokes it.*)

As a matter of fact, it makes my painting better.

MIRANDA: Let's just get on with mopping, shall we?

(*MIRANDA takes the bucket that ANGELA wrote on off-stage.*)

If we don't finish before she gets back she'll say I've been leading her 'little baby kangaroo' astray.

TITUS: Don't call me baby kangaroo.

(*MIRANDA comes back with water in the bucket.*)

MIRANDA: Okay baby kangaroo, you mop over there –

TITUS: I said don't call me that.

MIRANDA: And I'll mop over here. Baby kangaroo.

(*They start mopping.*)

TITUS: I know something that you don't know. A tiger's paw print is actually called a pug mark.

MIRANDA: Who doesn't know that?

TITUS: And tiger stripes are like fingerprints, because no two tigers have exactly the same pattern. And the heaviest tiger ever weighed was four hundred and sixty-six kilograms. Fourteen times the size of a girl like you.

MIRANDA: There.

TITUS: What?

MIRANDA: I've written 'explosion' on the floor with my mop.

(*TITUS looks.*)

TITUS: There's no z in explosion, pebble brain.

MIRANDA: There's no z in shut your mouth either.

(*They mop.*)

TITUS: Did you know that a tiger marks out its territory with its own wee? That and other special smells –

MIRANDA: Will you shut up about tigers and mop?!

TITUS: I am mopping!

MIRANDA: Saturdays are for shopping and mucking about, not for mopping floors and taking medicine. Why mop the floor on a Saturday?

TITUS: You know exactly why. Saturday's the day when all the insects of the world gather their food. One tiny breadcrumb could attract a plague of cockroaches.

MIRANDA: That's a bag of cobblers.

TITUS: Is not. She said so when we were fixing the fence.

MIRANDA: I know she said so. I know she said so. But don't you ever imagine for one tiny pea-brained moment that she might be telling lies? Don't you ever wonder for one teeny thick-headed moment whether all these stories might just be a pile of porkies?

(*Short pause.*)

TITUS: Why would she make things up?

MIRANDA: Don't ask me. Maybe she's some kind of crackpot.

TITUS: You shut up.

MIRANDA: Maybe she's some kind of cuckoo-head.

TITUS: You shut your ungrateful mouth. Maybe you're the cuckoo-head.

MIRANDA: Face it, Titus. The rules make about as much sense as a cow in a rabbit hutch.

TITUS: You're just grumpy because you've got to drink the medicine. Or is it because you're frightened by your stupid dream which I bet you didn't even have.

MIRANDA: I wasn't frightened by it. Nothing frightens me.

(*MIRANDA begins mopping near the microwave.*)

TITUS: Don't go so near the microwave.

MIRANDA: Why not?

TITUS: Don't play games, you know why not. The air there makes our stomachs swell and makes our heartbeats weaker.

MIRANDA: Grow a brain. If that was really honestly true they wouldn't even make microwaves.

TITUS: I seriously believe you should move away –

MIRANDA: The Government would make laws against microwaves. Before I had to come and live in this loony house I stood by microwaves all the time. I virtually lived by microwaves.

TITUS: Don't lie.

MIRANDA: I'm not the fibber round here. Normal people in the normal world break these rules all the time. So why is it then, when we look out into the street, that we do not see people with swollen stomachs or lobster claws, or bad eyes from staring up at the sun...

(*MIRANDA picks up a household object. On the bottom it says 'Don't wear yellow socks.'*)

...or giant feet from wearing yellow socks? Because she makes the whole lot up, that's why!

TITUS: If you can't say anything sensible about the world –

MIRANDA: It's driving me mad!

TITUS: You might as well shut your face!

MIRANDA: Deal with it. She lies. She's a strange and messed-up bully that takes everything out on us. Before my entire life went haywire I was allowed to grow my hair and clip my toenails. My Mum and Dad let me sing in the bath and put posters on the wall and spin in circles until I got dizzy and have a pattern on my duvet and whisper and wink and burp and skip and have kippers for flipping well breakfast!!!

TITUS: Then maybe you're lucky they died when they did.

(*Pause. MIRANDA takes an egg from the egg holding ornament. She shows it to TITUS.*)

MIRANDA: One egg.

TITUS: What are you doing?

MIRANDA: I'm going to smash it.

TITUS: Don't be ridiculous. I didn't mean to say that.

MIRANDA: I am, I'm going to smash it.

TITUS: Stop that now, Miranda. You know exactly what happens when you break an egg. Your body goes all egg-shaped and your skin goes hard and cracks apart.

MIRANDA: I think we should see about that.

(*TITUS begins to slowly creep towards MIRANDA with his arms outstretched.*)

TITUS: I'd like you to put the egg down and leave the area in a calm and sensible manner. Gently on the floor now.

(*MIRANDA slowly crouches down as if she is planning to place the egg on the floor gently.*)

That's it. Easy as we go. No heroics.

(*The egg reaches an inch from the floor. MIRANDA looks up and smiles at TITUS, then tosses the egg high into the air. They watch it fall to the floor and smash. MIRANDA hugs herself and smiles a broad and contented smile.*)

Fabulous, Miranda, that's gone and done it. That's really gone and done it, that has. How very extremely clever you seem to be. I'll just stand and watch you go all egg-shaped, shall I?

(*TITUS marches around MIRANDA looking for signs of change.*)

Bye then, Miranda. It was nice knowing you before you went egg-shaped.

MIRANDA: It feels fantastic, Titus. It feels like melted chocolate.

TITUS: Yeah, until your skin goes hard and cracks apart. What a brilliant decision you just made.

MIRANDA: My skin feels fine.

TITUS: What a way to go.

MIRANDA: Nothing is happening to my skin and I am not going egg-shaped. She has been stringing us a silly bag of lies.

TITUS: Maybe it doesn't kick in for a moment or two.

MIRANDA: Face facts, it's all a total sack of trumped-up fairy stories. Okay, close your eyes and hold out your hand.

TITUS: What for?

MIRANDA: What's the matter gutless chicken, scared of the dark?

(*TITUS makes a show of how fearlessly he can close his eyes and put out his hand. MIRANDA takes another egg from the holder and puts it in TITUS' hand.*)

Are you ready for absolute pleasure?

(*TITUS opens his eyes and fixes a stare on the egg. He fixes a desperate stare on it.*)

TITUS: Take it away.

MIRANDA: It feels like melted chocolate, honestly it does.

TITUS: You're just scared of being the only egg-shaped one round here.

MIRANDA: You're just scared of what mummy might say if little baby kangaroo broke a little baby rule.

TITUS: I'm not scared, I'm just bored of the whole thing.

MIRANDA: Don't lie to me. You're dying to feel the crunchy shell crunching in your hand like a giant's hand. And all that stringy splidgey egg all oozing through your fingers.

TITUS: Don't you ever shut up?

MIRANDA: If only you had the guts.

TITUS: Nothing to do with guts in the slightest.

MIRANDA: What a miracle! Miranda still hasn't turned into an egg! Absolutely no good reason for Titus not to smash one too. Unless, of course, he's a total chicken chicken scared-of-mummy yellow-belly scaredy-cat.

TITUS: A rule is a rule is a rule is a –

MIRANDA: Pathetic. What a hero!

TITUS: I am behaving responsibly!

MIRANDA: What a brave tiger! Can't even break an egg! You're nothing like a tiger or an eagle. You're just a brainless baby kangaroo that hides in Mummy's pouch! A brainless baby –

TITUS: I'm warning you!

MIRANDA: Pathetic baby kangaroo –

TITUS: Stop it now!

MIRANDA: Brainless baby kangaroo that hides in Mummy's pouch!

(*TITUS makes a surprisingly manly screaming sound and crushes the egg in his hand. Astonished at himself, he drops the shell to the floor and watches as the strands of egg white hang from his fingers. He puts his clean hand to his face.)*

TITUS: My skin's going hard. My glands are swelling. Feel my face, it's cracking up!

(MIRANDA grabs TITUS' face roughly.)

MIRANDA: Perfectly normal skin.

TITUS: Really?

MIRANDA: Honest. So go on then, how did it feel?

TITUS: It felt…magnificent! Melted chocolate.

MIRANDA: Didn't I say?

(A distant flash of lightning.)

TITUS: When the shell went crack my whole guts went round the bend. Energy bubbles rushing through me. And the crunching noise and the sticky yolk in my paws, it made me feel so…powerful!

(MIRANDA places the washing up bowl on the table. 'No hiding of toothbrushes' is on the side of it, freshly painted.)

Strength from my toes to the tips of my whiskers!

(A distant rumble of thunder.)

What was that noise?!

MIRANDA: Just a bit of thunder. Hey Titus.

(MIRANDA pours some milk into the washing up bowl.)

TITUS: What are you doing?

MIRANDA: I am making one massive mixture.

TITUS: You are joking me, Miranda.

MIRANDA: I'm going to put milk, peas, toothpaste, beer, sticks, make-up, paint and washing up liquid in this bowl, and then I'm going to squidge it all about.

(MIRANDA exits purposefully. TITUS peers into the bowl.)

TITUS: Just because you were right about the egg rule, that doesn't mean that they're all invented. That could just be a blip in the system. And you know what she said would happen if we ever made a mixture. She said our insides would gradually jumble until our hearts were in our heads and our brains were in our chests. That's what she said.

(*MIRANDA comes back with toothpaste, sticks, beer and make-up.*)

MIRANDA: That's a sack of twaddle and you know it.

TITUS: I don't know what I know any more.

(*TITUS joins MIRANDA by the mixing bowl.*)

MIRANDA: I think I'll call it…Miranda's Mishmash Gloop.

(*MIRANDA squeezes toothpaste in and adds peas and beer.*)

A scientific potion for stomach pains and verrucas. Stick some washing-up liquid in.

(*TITUS nervously adds washing up liquid then feels his chest.*)

That's the boy.

(*MIRANDA adds the following…*)

And some paint. And some sticks. And some make-up. And a handful of water for good measure. And then squidge the whole lot up.

(*MIRANDA squidges her Mishmash Gloop about.*)

Plunge in and feel it, Titus.

TITUS: No thanks.

MIRANDA: Don't be a baby, stick your hands in.

(*MIRANDA grabs TITUS' hands and puts them in the mix.*)

TITUS: Miranda! Ooh, that feels good.

(*They squidge the mixture about, lifting handfuls from the bowl then watching it gooily plop back in.*)

MIRANDA: I used to make at least one mixture a week. Once I made skin cream with rose petals and mayonnaise and sold it to a neighbour for five pounds sixty.

TITUS: Get lost you never.

MIRANDA: It made her look ten years younger and she wasn't that old in the first place. I think I'll open the Animal's cage.

(*MIRANDA wipes her hands on her clothes, goes to the Animal's cage and opens it.*)

Poor old sick old Animal, locked up all day long. Much rather have some lovely old space to scamper round in, wouldn't you? I'll leave the cage open, you may come and go as you please.

TITUS: If any harm comes to him, you'll be on the chopping block.

MIRANDA: Don't be such a whingeing little square.

TITUS: Just a friendly warning.

MIRANDA: Yeah well, one more friendly warning and you'll be on the chopping block and I'll be chopping.

(*MIRANDA starts banging a plastic spoon on the table rhythmically. A closer flash of lightning and a louder rumble of thunder.*)

TITUS: Don't bang plastic spoons, Miranda –

(*MIRANDA presses the spoon against TITUS' mouth, holds it there a moment, then bangs a few more times and sings…*)

MIRANDA: Breakfast! Breakfast!

TITUS: No making up songs about breakfast –

(*She presses the spoon against his mouth again, holds it there a moment, then resumes banging and singing.*)

MIRANDA: Breakfast! Breakfast!

(*TITUS attempts to wrestle the spoon from MIRANDA's hand. He succeeds, but finds that she is now playing with a spoon in her other hand and that he is banging the spoon independently. He cannot stop himself.*)

What shall we have for breakfast?

Toasted crumpets and marmalade,

Stick it all in my mouth mouth mouth mouth.

(*Gradually MIRANDA becomes more raucous and TITUS begins to enjoy the song.*)

Breakfast. Breakfast.

What shall we have for breakfast?

Smoked kippers and yoghurt and stuff,

Stuff it all in my gob gob gob gob.

(*MIRANDA picks up a mop with her spare hand and uses it like a microphone.*)

Breakfast. Breakfast.

What do you want for your breakfast?

(*She puts the microphone mop in TITUS' direction.*)

TITUS: Sausages, sausages, sausages

And a runny fried egg and a cup of tea.

MIRANDA: A runny fried egg and a cup of tea. *(She burps.)*

TITUS: A runny fried egg and a cup of tea. (*He burps.*)

TITUS / MIRANDA: A runny fried egg and a cup of tea. (*They burp.*)

Breakfast breakfast

What shall we have for breakfast?

MIRANDA: Cereal with nuts and stuff.

TITUS: Beans on toast with mushrooms in.

MIRANDA: Pancakes with bananas on.

TITUS: Bread with bits of chocolate in

All crammed in my mouth mouth mouth mouth.

TITUS / MIRANDA: Mouth mouth mouth mouth

Mouth mouth mouth mouth

Mouth mouth mouth mouth.

MIRANDA: All through the wintertime

She made them just eat peas.

TITUS: Then she went away and left us here

And we very soon agreed

TITUS / MIRANDA: We'll have a very fine breakfast indeed.

(*TITUS takes a handful of Mishmash Gloop.*)

MIRANDA: Breakfast breakfast

Mouth mouth mouth mouth

Mouth mouth mouth mouth

Breakfast…

(*TITUS throws the Gloop and it splats on MIRANDA.*)

I'll get you for that. I'll splat you for that.

(*MIRANDA gets a handful and throws it at TITUS. A Gloop battle ensues. MIRANDA gains the upper hand and TITUS scarpers. She chases him as he darts about the room and under the table. For a moment he hides and she loses him…*)

I know exactly where you are.

(*TITUS pops up and throws a banana at MIRANDA. The chase begins again and she has nearly caught him when he grabs a mop. A closer flash of lightning.*)

TITUS: On guard, foolish challenger!

(*MIRANDA grabs the other mop.*)

MIRANDA: On guard, potato-brained warrior!

(*A louder rumble of thunder and the sound of rain outside begins.*)

TITUS: I have slain a thousand dragons with the mop you see before you. I don't imagine a girl will prove too difficult.

(*TITUS swings his mop twice but MIRANDA defends well.*)

MIRANDA: Think again, foolish mop-swinger! I'm just as strong as any boy and twenty times more nimble.

TITUS: As nimble as a hippo, perhaps!

(*TITUS swings his mop twice more, again defended well.*)

MIRANDA: Did a feather brush my sword?!

TITUS: Indeed! A feather of death!

(*MIRANDA goes on the attack and TITUS defends.*)

Indeed you are as nimble as a kitten. But how can you cope with the strength of a tiger?!

(*TITUS lunges with his mop. MIRANDA dodges and grabs the other end of it. They swing themselves once round clockwise making a 'whoa' sound, then once round anti-clockwise making an 'aaah' sound.*)

MIRANDA: I'm going to play some music and dance.

TITUS: No way am I dancing.

MIRANDA: Please your stupid self.

(*She lets go of the mop, causing TITUS to fall on his bum.*)

Whoops-a-daisy!

(*She goes off. He picks himself up, goes to the table and uses his mop like a snooker cue to poke something. Classical music begins to play loudly. Captured by the music, TITUS begins to scatter handfuls of peas in a ceremonious way. MIRANDA comes back on.*)

MIRANDA: Your Mum's music is such a sack of junk. Who plays records any more?

(*TITUS scatters some peas on MIRANDA's head. With great seriousness she begins dancing in a strange half-ballet-half-girl-band style, trying to account for every mood and twist in the music. A closer flash of lightning and a louder rumble of thunder. As she dances she makes even more mess, knocking stools over and messing up anything else around. TITUS throws peas everywhere. He then tires of pea throwing and decides to conduct the music. Seamlessly he changes from conducting the music to copying MIRANDA's dance routine. A closer flash of lightning and a louder rumble of thunder. To MIRANDA's increasing annoyance, they keep bumping into each other. MIRANDA wrestles TITUS to the ground then straightens her clothes and continues the routine. A closer flash of lightning and a louder rumble of thunder. TITUS crawls back to the table, pretending to be a caterpillar. He climbs onto it and stirs the Gloop with his mop. A flash of lightning very nearby and a very loud rumble of thunder. He picks out a stick and conducts. He sees the bottle of beer on the table and picks it up. As he swigs it, ANGELA walks into the room. She is wet from the rain. She holds a bottle of medicine. She is utterly, utterly horrified at what she sees. She screams a peculiar scream. There is an almighty flash and crash as lightning strikes the house. The light-bulbs blow and the off-stage record player blows up. In the dim eclipse-like light, MIRANDA runs at ANGELA and pushes her over...*)

You liar!!!

(*MIRANDA stands over ANGELA for a short moment, then leaves...*)

ANGELA: Miranda, come back!

(*Pause.*)

Titus. Help me. Give me your hand.

(*TITUS does not move.*)

Titus? Titus? Baby Kangaroo?

(*TITUS leaves.*)

Please come back. Both of you. It really isn't safe. Please…
Please! You're my pair of perfect peas in a pod.

(*ANGELA crawls to the table. She mumbles as she crawls.*)

Oh my goodness… Something terrible will happen… I
know it will… I know it will… Please don't let something
terrible happen…

(*ANGELA uses the table to get herself back on her feet. She lights
the candle.*)

You understand don't you, Animal? I only make the rules
to be kind. Only to protect you all from danger.

(*ANGELA holds the candle up to the cage.*)

You wouldn't survive ten minutes without your special
cage and diet, would you, Animal? Animal, where are you?

(*ANGELA sobs.*)

End of Act One.)

ACT TWO

SCENE ONE

(*Twilight hangs and shadows loom across a grassless patch of land on the edge of a wood quite far from anywhere. Four tree stumps, irregularly spaced, poke out of the ground. A pile of blackened twigs and ash, surrounded by a circle of stones and boulders, sits in the centre of this eerie place. Some branches and a grimy plastic sheet are strewn across the ground. Weird sounds and nasty shadows inhabit this place.*

ANGELA enters, looks around and feels a chill run down her spine. She calls out and her voice echoes creepily.)

ANGELA: Titus. Miranda. Please come out if you're hiding. This place, it really doesn't feel safe. You caught me by surprise, that's all. Please come out. You're my pair of perfect peas in a pod…

(*Pause.*)

I never told you what happens to children that run away. It's a terrible thing. Their bodies slowly turn into shadows. And not just normal shadows. Terribly long, cold, sad ones. And bats and field-mice live inside their heads. And their knees make noises like creaking windmills. And their eyeballs turn to ice-blocks and their tongues go hard and black. But that's only if they stay out all night. Please come home. Come home and we'll forget you ever did it.

(*ANGELA moves on. An owl hoots. Very faintly, an unseen woman sings in a sad and distant way. A mysterious shadow passes across the stage. TITUS and MIRANDA walk into the space. TITUS is very scared.*)

TITUS: What was that?

MIRANDA: What?

TITUS: I saw something move.

MIRANDA: Probably a shadow of a branch. Where are we?

TITUS: Wherever it is, it's making my blood freeze.

MIRANDA: Some tiger you'd make.

TITUS: Get lost Miranda, even a tiger would have found that forest spooky. And this place is hardly any better. My spine feels like an icicle.

(*MIRANDA stops walking and TITUS walks round in circles.*)

MIRANDA: It's getting really dark –

TITUS: Don't remind me!

MIRANDA: Maybe we should set up camp for the night.

TITUS: Is that some kind of joke? I would much rather keep walking if it's all the same to you. Every time I stop it's like a ghost walks through my body.

MIRANDA: But we can't keep walking forever. My feet are getting blisters and we need to save our energy.

TITUS: If we just keep going until morning we'll be –

MIRANDA: Stand still, Titus!

(*TITUS stands still.*)

I've made a decision and we're setting up camp here. I am the oldest.

TITUS: Here?

MIRANDA: It's perfect.

TITUS: It's the creepiest place in the universe.

MIRANDA: But there's stumps to sit on, look. And a fireplace for fires. And the view across the field is fairly…

TITUS: Spine-chilling. I am not being funny, but the air round here is weirdly cold and there is something about these shadows –

MIRANDA: Stop being such a thick-headed baby.

TITUS: Okay then, what if someone still lives here? And what if they find us on their patch of ground?

MIRANDA: Nobody lives here.

TITUS: Well someone lit a fire.

(*TITUS begins walking round in circles again.*)

MIRANDA: Years ago, probably. We'll stay here for tonight, okay? If in the morning it still doesn't feel like home, we'll go and find somewhere else. If we decide we like it, we can stay forever.

TITUS: I'd rather live in Dracula's castle.

MIRANDA: You're making me dizzy, Titus. Why don't you lie down and have a rest? Take a few deep breaths.

TITUS: What, sleep down there with wolves and weasels sniffing round my feet? And spiders lowering themselves onto my face? You're even madder than I thought.

MIRANDA: Why don't you stick up a tent then?

(*TITUS stops.*)

TITUS: If I had a tent to stick up that's exactly what I'd do.

MIRANDA: Build one then. Build one with the stuff that's lying round.

TITUS: If you can tell me how to build a tent with the stuff in this complete empty nightmare of a place, I'll give you a million pounds.

MIRANDA: Okay. There's a plastic sheet down there. And some branches and some stones. And there was a traffic cone a little way back. Stick the stick in the ground and the sheet on top, prop it up with the cone and weight it down with the stones.

TITUS: You know I haven't got a million pounds.

(*TITUS goes to fetch the traffic cone. As he goes…*)

If you're so clever, I don't know why you can't build it.

MIRANDA: I'm not the kangaroo that wants a tent. I'm at my happiest gazing up at the stars.

(*Now alone, MIRANDA lets her guard down slightly. She picks up a couple of stones and lobs them at a tree stump. The faint singing voice is heard again, apparently coming from the tree stump. Puzzled and scared, MIRANDA moves towards the tree stump. The singing fades away. TITUS returns with a traffic cone.*)

Was that you singing?

TITUS: What have I got to sing about?

MIRANDA: I thought I heard a voice. It was creepy.

(*TITUS begins to build the tent.*)

Hey Titus, maybe this place is haunted.

TITUS: Shut your stupid mouth.

MIRANDA: Maybe a man-eating monster lives here. Or the ghost of The Lady In White. Have you heard of The Lady In White?

TITUS: You think you're hilarious but you're actually extremely boring –

MIRANDA: She was drowned in the lake on a freezing night by her evil cowardly husband. Now she haunts all cowards for revenge, attacking them when they least expect it.

TITUS: You'd better watch out then.

MIRANDA: Or this could be the home of the vicious one-legged zombie.

(*MIRANDA begins to hop around with arms outstretched zombie-style.*)

He died of shock when his leg fell off and he turned into a zombie. Now he hops around the world with his eyes wide open and his arms stretched out, and he zombifies the people that he meets.

TITUS: My head is actually aching with boredom.

MIRANDA: Or the spirit of Seven-Eyed Jack. Or The Phantom Body Snatcher! Or the ghost that has the head of a goat but the body of a school teacher! This could be where she lives –

TITUS: You're not being funny so you might as well belt your mouth up!

MIRANDA: Or The Mouth Collector from my dream.

(*TITUS finishes the tent. It's not up to much.*)

TITUS: There, I've finished. What do you think?

(*MIRANDA inspects the tent from a variety of angles. She moves one of the stones a fraction and steps back to admire her handiwork.*)

MIRANDA: Perfect. What a team. Now, let's sit down and enjoy our new life.

(*They sit. Long pause.*)

TITUS: Aren't you even slightly scared, Miranda?

(*Short pause.*)

MIRANDA: Don't be such a weakling, there's nothing to be scared of.

(*Long pause.*)

This is fun.

TITUS: It's about as much fun as an ear infection.

MIRANDA: Don't be so negative.

TITUS: An ear infection on a windy day.

(*Pause.*)

And much less safe.

MIRANDA: Are you hungry?

TITUS: Yes. I could eat a rhinoceros.

MIRANDA: I've got a biscuit.

TITUS: Why didn't you say before?

MIRANDA: Do you want half or not?

(*MIRANDA takes a foil-wrapped biscuit from somewhere on her person.*)

I thought we could have it as a midnight feast, but all that walking made me dead hungry.

TITUS: Hurry up.

(*TITUS holds out his hand. MIRANDA looks into the foil and is disappointed.*)

MIRANDA: Oh.

(*She pours some biscuit crumbs into TITUS' hand.*)

It must have got crushed when I slipped on that dead hedgehog.

(*TITUS brushes his hands clean disdainfully and sulks.*)

MIRANDA: Cheer up. You look like you've swallowed a miserable frog.

TITUS: No food, no comfortable furniture. Ghosts. No radiators –

MIRANDA: No exact bedtime, no mopping, no dusting, no watering the pea patch or speaking French on Tuesdays. No-one telling you when you can paint. If Titus wants to paint a picture, Titus paints a flipping picture!

TITUS: I didn't even bring any brushes.

MIRANDA: We can buy brushes.

TITUS: What with?

MIRANDA: Come on, don't be like that. This is freedom at last. And it might take a little tiny bit of getting used to, but freedom is honestly a massive sack of fun.

TITUS: Is it?

MIRANDA: Think how much fun we were having before Old Strict Knickers came back. It's going to be like that all the time. There's only one rule in this joint and that's that there are no rules. Okay?

TITUS: This joint makes me feel sick.

MIRANDA: Never mind that, what shall we do first?

TITUS: I don't know.

MIRANDA: You choose. Anything.

TITUS: I suppose we could…run about.

MIRANDA: That is a brilliant idea.

(MIRANDA jumps up and helps a less enthusiastic TITUS to his feet.)

Okay then, let's run over there!

(They run to the place and stop.)

Over there now!

(With a bit less enthusiasm, they run to the place and stop. Short pause.)

Back over there?

(They jog half-heartedly back to their starting place. Pause as they contemplate despair.)

TITUS: We could have a swordfight like before if we had mops.

(MIRANDA sees a branch on the ground and grabs it.)

MIRANDA: On guard, potato-brained warrior.

(*TITUS grabs one too.*)

TITUS: On guard, foolish challenger. I've slain a thousand dragons with the branch you see before you. Prepare for something ferocious.

MIRANDA: 'I don't imagine a girl will prove too difficult.'

TITUS: What?

MIRANDA: That's what you say.

TITUS: I was doing it different.

MIRANDA: Well do it the same!

TITUS: Okay. I don't imagine a girl will prove too difficult.

(*TITUS swings his mop twice but MIRANDA defends well.*)

MIRANDA: Think again, foolish mop-swinger! I'm just as strong as any boy and twenty times more nimble.

TITUS: As nimble as…an elephant, perhaps!

MIRANDA: No.

TITUS: A cow perhaps!

MIRANDA: No.

TITUS: A…badger perhaps?

MIRANDA: Hippo!

TITUS: Sorry. Hippo perhaps!

(*TITUS swings his mop twice more, again defended well.*)

MIRANDA: Did a feather brush my sword?!

TITUS: A feather?

MIRANDA: A feather of death!

(*MIRANDA goes on a ferocious attack and TITUS defends.*)

TITUS: I know this bit. You are as nimble as a tiger. But how can you cope with the strength of a kitten?!

MIRANDA: The other way around!

(*Baffled, TITUS turns to face the other way.*)

TITUS: You are as nimble as a tiger. But how can you cope –

MIRANDA: This is the worst swordfight in history!!!

(*MIRANDA throws her branch down in frustration.*)

TITUS: I can't concentrate. This place –

MIRANDA: What have you got in your head?! A dead gerbil?!

TITUS: No.

MIRANDA: A brain made out of tiger poo?!

TITUS: Let's just do something else.

MIRANDA: All right. All right, let's smash up the tent. Let's trample this idiotic tent up!

TITUS: We can't. We'll have nowhere –

(*MIRANDA begins to trample. TITUS tries to stop her.*)

MIRANDA: We can do whatever we like –

TITUS: Miranda –

MIRANDA: No flipping rules if I remember correctly.

TITUS: Miranda! Have your brains fallen out or something?! Miranda!

(*MIRANDA finishes trampling.*)

MIRANDA: There.

TITUS: That is the dimmest, dumbest, thickest, stupidest thing that anybody ever did in the history of mankind. We've got nowhere to sleep.

MIRANDA: I don't terribly care.

TITUS: There could be man-eating monsters round here. And there could be ghosts. And there could be fierce animals. That is not my cup of tea.

MIRANDA: Your voice is like a squeaky blackboard.

TITUS: Never smash our shared things up again, all right?!

MIRANDA: All right!

TITUS: That's a rule!

MIRANDA: Fine!

TITUS: The sheet's all torn now. Go and find another.

(*MIRANDA leaves. Thunder rumbles.*)

SCENE TWO

(*ANGELA walks along a hill path, carrying a rucksack. Nearby, Animal sits on a rock.*)

ANGELA: And your eyebrows grow right round your face. And your fingers turn bright blue. And every time you close your eyes, you see witches and goblins and gravestones and…

(*Exhausted, ANGELA stops to look out across the town.*)

Please come home. The world's not safe and I think a storm's brewing up. And remember, it's Saturday night. That means a slice of banana cake for tea. Please come home.

(*She decides to rest on the rock. She sits on Animal and Animal squeaks. She jumps up and sees him.*)

Animal? Is that you?

(*She looks closer.*)

The scab in the shape of a violin! It is you! You squeaked! I thought without your cage that you'd be dead within an hour. Without your heating lamp and special diet. Your teeth, they're sharp again. You're eyes are like emeralds. And the strength of your legs! What have you been eating?!

ANGELA picks up Animal and holds him close to her face.)

I've been stupid, Animal. I've been stupid, haven't I?

SCENE THREE

(*The camp is under siege from a thunder storm. It is so dark that nothing can be seen, but howling wind, lashing rain, rumbling thunder and screaming TITUS can be heard.*)

TITUS: Miranda! Miranda! We're being blown away!

(*Three flashes of lightning reveal TITUS in various scenarios of windswept panic. Suddenly, the storm subsides and some light falls on the scene. TITUS is wet, baffled and bedraggled. The sound of the singing woman returns.*)

Hello?

(*TITUS looks around in search of the sound's source, eventually realising that it comes from one of the tree stumps. Tentatively, he approaches the stump.*)

Hello? Are you trapped in there? Is there anything I can do to help? I've got a tool box at home but… Please stop singing.

(*TITUS knocks on the stump. The singing gets louder.*)

Please stop, my nerves are jangling. There's nothing I can do.

(*The singing gets louder. TITUS knocks on the stump.*)

I don't understand what you want! Just stop it! Please stop!

(*TITUS bangs hard on the top of the stump and it flips open to reveal a secret compartment. The singing becomes louder and unmuffled. TITUS peers inside. Terrified but curious, he reaches into the stump and takes out a picture frame. The singing fades away as he looks at the picture. He speaks into it.*)

Hello?

(*A female figure, swathed all in white, walks silently into the space, unseen by TITUS. She stretches a hand out towards TITUS in a mysterious and menacing way. A crow caws. TITUS feels the presence of the swathed figure. He turns slowly to face her. She looks at him. He is gripped with fear.*)

The Lady In White.

(*Suddenly, she rushes at TITUS with her arms outstretched. He dodges her first lunge, but she soon catches him.*)

There must be some mistake! Let go of me!!!

(*He breaks free and grabs a branch. He swipes the branch at her twice, but she evades it skilfully. He takes an almighty third swing, misses again and overbalances. While he is face-down on the ground, she hides. He gets up and can't see her.*)

I know you're still here, I can hear you breathing. Miranda will be back in a minute and she'll… Miranda! Come back here a minute! Please!

(*The swathed figure creeps out from her hiding place, still unseen by TITUS.*)

There's something that I really need some help with!

(*She pounces on TITUS and pins him to the ground. He whimpers and wails pathetically.*)

I'm not a coward, so please don't hurt me. Please, I'm begging you please.

(*She begins to laugh.*)

Miranda! Help! It's The Lady In White! It's The Lady In White!

(*Continuing to laugh, The Lady In White uncovers her face to reveal her true identity: it is MIRANDA. Short pause as MIRANDA smiles and TITUS realises MIRANDA's trick.*)

You cruel idiot.

MIRANDA: (*Mocking.*) 'I'm not a coward so please don't hurt me.'

TITUS: That is the most spiteful thing –

MIRANDA: What a tiger!

TITUS: If you think that's funny you need your brain looking into.

MIRANDA: It was only a bit of spooking around.

TITUS: I thought I was dead. My whole life flashed up in front of me.

MIRANDA: You put up a decent enough fight for a baby. I don't know why you're so upset.

TITUS: Because things are spooky enough without us spooking each other around! Okay?!

MIRANDA: Okay.

TITUS: No more spooking about!

MIRANDA: All right.

TITUS: Because I'm telling you, things are getting pretty flipping mind-boggling round here.

(*TITUS points out the picture frame.*)

Pictures in picture frames –

MIRANDA: Where did that come from?

TITUS: You won't believe me but it came from that tree stump.

MIRANDA: Get lost.

TITUS: Honestly.

(*MIRANDA picks up the picture and looks at it. It makes her smile and be sad.*)

MIRANDA: Look at the picture. The baby's eyes are bluer than anything. And the Mummy's smile. They all look so completely…

(*The sound of a baby crying comes from a different tree stump.*)

Can you hear a baby crying?

TITUS: That's what I'm telling you. It's coming from a tree stump. While you were away I heard a woman. She was singing to herself in the tree stump.

MIRANDA: I heard a woman singing.

TITUS: So I went straight up and I banged on the stump and that's where I found the picture frame.

MIRANDA: The stump just opened up?

TITUS: Yes. When I banged it.

(*They listen to the baby crying.*)

MIRANDA: It's coming from that one.

(*MIRANDA puts the frame down lovingly on its stump. They creep towards the crying stump.*)

Open it then.

(*In expert fashion, TITUS puts his ear close to the top of the stump and listens to the hollow sound as he taps it lightly with two fingers. He then leans back and whacks it, flipping it open. The baby's crying becomes louder and clearer.*)

Is there a baby?

TITUS: It's a doll.

MIRANDA: Dolls don't cry like that. What kind of person leaves a baby in a tree stump?

TITUS: No, it's a doll.

(*TITUS pulls the doll from the tree stump. It is peculiar and beautiful, with a dark and shiny head, across which creeping vines are painted.*)

How can we make it stop?

MIRANDA: Hold her closer and pat her back. Poor thing, she's crying her lungs out.

(*Uncomfortably, TITUS holds the doll closer and pats her back.*)

TITUS: It doesn't feel like a living person. Just like a doll but softer.

MIRANDA: She smells all sweet like a baby though. She smells like sweet milk.

TITUS: It won't stop crying. My nerves are getting tense.

MIRANDA: You're not doing it properly. Give her to me.

(*TITUS passes the doll to MIRANDA.*)

TITUS: Things are getting dead, dead strange.

MIRANDA: I know.

TITUS: Maybe it's a sign. Maybe we should go back.

MIRANDA: I think she's cold. I think we should wrap her in the sheet. Lay it out flat.

(*TITUS lays the sheet out flat and MIRANDA places the doll down. As they wrap her up.*)

No need to cry, little one. You'll be as warm as toast. Make sure her feet are covered.

(*MIRANDA picks up the wrapped doll. The crying stops.*)

TITUS: What a relief! Right, I think we should probably go now. One more minute in this place –

MIRANDA: Go? We haven't even looked in the other two stumps.

TITUS: I think we should go all the same. It could be anything stuck in those stumps.

MIRANDA: Exactly. Like treasure or secrets or…food for the baby.

TITUS: It's not a baby, it's a scary doll! It doesn't have a stomach!

(*Short pause.*)

MIRANDA: We should still look. If we don't look we'll spend the rest of our lives wondering.

TITUS: If we have lives.

MIRANDA: Do you really want to walk back through the forest?

(*Short pause.*)

TITUS: Okay, but you bang it. I'm standing well back.

MIRANDA: Okay. Hold the baby.

TITUS: It's a doll.

MIRANDA: Carefully, she's asleep.

(*MIRANDA passes the doll to TITUS and approaches the third tree stump.*)

No noises this time.

(*MIRANDA bangs the top of the stump. It flips open and she looks in.*)

I can't see anything. Shall I put my hand in?

TITUS: Your choice.

(*Nervously, MIRANDA puts her hand in. She pulls out a miniature pair of striped pyjamas on a hanger.*)

MIRANDA: Those are the smallest pyjamas I have ever seen.

(*MIRANDA gently puts the pyjamas by the picture frame. She looks at the picture again.*)

TITUS: Is that it? A tiny pair of pyjamas?

MIRANDA: There might have been something else.

TITUS: Take this thing off me.

MIRANDA: The Dad's hands are five times the size of the baby's.

TITUS: This thing doesn't even have proper hands.

(*TITUS passes the baby over to MIRANDA. She holds it, still looking at the picture. TITUS goes to the third stump and pulls*) *out a mask, oddly similar to the doll with a haunting design that incorporates tiger stripes.)*

Mask. Look at this mask, Miranda. Tiger stripes. It's the strangest, most amazing…

(TITUS gives in to his desire to wear it.)

Look at me in the mask. It smells like something dead.

(TITUS looks back into the stump.)

There's more! There's a whole stack!

(TITUS pulls a stack of similar masks from the stump and looks at a couple. They all have different mouths. MIRANDA turns to look at TITUS. Horror and confusion spread across her face.)

MIRANDA: Titus.

TITUS: What?

MIRANDA: I've seen it before.

TITUS: What?

MIRANDA: That mask you're wearing, I know I have! It's so familiar, it makes me feel sick!

TITUS: Don't lie, where would you have seen –

MIRANDA: I don't know! I'm racking my brains but I can't remember!

TITUS: Maybe it's just your imagination.

MIRANDA: Whatever it is, it's making my blood cold.

TITUS: You're making my blood freeze.

(MIRANDA lays the baby down and looks at the masks, racking her brains. TITUS tries to take the mask off.)

Oh no. You are joking. It's stuck on my head, Miranda. The stinking thing's stuck on my head. I can't spend the rest of my life like this! It won't…budge!

(MIRANDA takes two green apples from the tree stump.)

MIRANDA: Fresh apples.

TITUS: What?!

MIRANDA: Two fresh green apples in the stump.

TITUS: Somehow I've lost my flipping appetite!

MIRANDA: Someone still lives here, Titus. They've only just been left here. Otherwise, they'd be rotten. That is someone's fireplace and these are someone's things!

(*Pause.*)

TITUS: Mustn't jump to conclusions.

MIRANDA: It's true.

(*Pause.*)

TITUS: We're going. Even through the forest –

MIRANDA: We are not going anywhere –

TITUS: This is not a game –

MIRANDA: If this idiot wants to live here, he can fight us for it.

TITUS: If we run as fast as we can –

MIRANDA: I am not running anywhere. I am sick to my guts of moving round from place to place.

TITUS: It could be some kind of murderer.

MIRANDA: What kind of murderer keeps pictures in frames?! Listen Titus, if those are his pyjamas we have nothing to be frightened of, do we? We'll stay and fight.

(*Pause.*)

TITUS: We don't even know what's in the fourth stump yet. It might be full of blood and bones.

MIRANDA: Okay. Open it.

TITUS: Why me?

MIRANDA: You're better at it.

(*TITUS moves to the fourth stump.*)

TITUS: This thing on my head!

MIRANDA: We'll sort it out later.

(*TITUS bangs on the top of the stump but nothing happens. He bangs again and nothing happens. He sees that this stump is different and removes the entire top section of the stump to reveal a peculiar rabbit, similar in some ways to Animal and in other ways to the doll and the mask, with ears three feet long. TITUS laughs nervously, hysterically.*)

It's not funny.

TITUS: Look at the size of them!

MIRANDA: No Titus –

TITUS: I bet it can hear Australia!

MIRANDA: Put it back!

TITUS: What?

MIRANDA: I said put it back!

(*TITUS replaces the top part of the stump.*)

TITUS: Who's the chicken now? It's only a rabbit.

MIRANDA: That rabbit is the rabbit of The Mouth Collector.

TITUS: What?

MIRANDA: The mouth-stealing man in my dreams. That is his
   rabbit and those are his special masks. That's his family in
   the picture, his wife and baby that disappeared. This is his
   secret home that's like a spider's web!

TITUS: We are going.

MIRANDA: No.

TITUS: I value my mouth, Miranda!

MIRANDA: I know we can beat him.

TITUS: I don't even want to see him.

MIRANDA: You can't run away from The Mouth Collector!
   He just keeps catching up! I'll stay and guard. Go and find
   some decent weapons. Something with a spike.

(*MIRANDA shakes TITUS by the shoulders.*)

Come on Titus, be brave.

(*TITUS leaves. MIRANDA stands on guard. A rumble of thunder.
She hears a twig snap.*)

MIRANDA: Is there anybody there? Anybody?

(*The doll lets out a little cry. MIRANDA comforts it without
picking it up.*)

It's okay, baby. It's okay, little one.

(*The doll stops crying. MIRANDA hears another noise. She moves
away from the doll.*)

Is there anybody there?

(*THE MOUTH COLLECTOR walks into the space. He wears a mask similar to the one stuck on TITUS' head, and similar clothes. MIRANDA mistakes him for TITUS.*)

Titus! You haven't got anything! You haven't even looked!

(*Frantic, furious and ashamed, THE MOUTH COLLECTOR goes to his special things. He hugs the doll tightly, then puts the scattered masks and the pyjamas back into stumps.*)

Titus, what are you doing? Stop it. Leave that stuff alone, we need weapons! This is a state of emergency!

(*TITUS comes back.*)

TITUS: I can't find anything. We'll have to use branches.

(*MIRANDA screams. THE MOUTH COLLECTOR looks at MIRANDA.*)

MIRANDA: The Mouth Collector.

(*THE MOUTH COLLECTOR moves towards MIRANDA. He comes behind her and takes hold of her, one hand over her mouth.*)

TITUS: Let go of her, Mouth Collector. Let go of her now.

(*THE MOUTH COLLECTOR stands firm.*)

You don't frighten me, Mouth Collector. Creeping up on people at night, you're more of a coward than me. Just let go.

(*Pause.*)

We know about your wife and baby, and we're sorry about that, but no amount of stolen mouths will ever bring them back, so let go.

(*Pause.*)

Let go now or I will fight you, Mouth Collector. I mean it, I'll fight you. I will fight you and fight you and I will not give up, so you might as well let go of her now or I'll fight you, Mouth Collector. People's mouths belong on people's faces, now let go of her this instant!!

(*The strength of TITUS' voice makes the doll cry.*)

Take your baby and leave us alone!!

113

(*THE MOUTH COLLECTOR grabs the doll and runs away. TITUS stands, emotionally drained, astonished by his own bravery. MIRANDA checks that her mouth is still stuck to her face.*)

MIRANDA: You did it… You did it, Titus! You saved my mouth!

TITUS: I did it.

MIRANDA: That was, like, as brave as anyone's been in the history of the world. You even scared me you were so frightening!

TITUS: I was brave.

MIRANDA: Brave as a tiger! 'People's mouths belong on people's faces, Mouth Collector! Let go of her this instant!' If there's one thing you are not it's a baby kangaroo!

(*MIRANDA starts to re-arrange the things that are lying around.*)

Well, that's the last we'll be seeing of that Mouth Collector, that's one thing for certain. This is our home now, Titus. It's going to be perfect. I'm sick of moving round from place to place. It's all ours!

TITUS: I wouldn't be so sure.

MIRANDA: What do you mean?

TITUS: He's coming back.

(*TITUS points at an approaching figure in the distance.*)

MIRANDA: Maybe it's just a shadow from the branches.

TITUS: I don't think so. It's coming this way and it's got a head and legs.

MIRANDA: Then we'll beat him again.

(*TITUS looks a bit doubtful.*)

Titus, we can do it! Quick, let's hide down by that tree stump, then when he comes we can rush at him together.

(*They hide.*)

TITUS: He looks pretty angry. And he's carrying a bag.

MIRANDA: Be careful. It's probably full of snakes or something.

114

TITUS: Probably snakes with fangs like knives!

MIRANDA: As long as we stick together…

(*They wait in nervous silence for a few seconds. MIRANDA counts down from three with her fingers. A hooded figure walks into the space. TITUS and MIRANDA scream, run and push the intruder over. The hood falls away to reveal ANGELA. Animal's head is poking out of the top of her backpack, unharmed.*)

MIRANDA: Angela?

ANGELA: Miranda!

TITUS: Mum?

ANGELA: Titus, is that you?

TITUS: It's stuck on my head. I can't get it off.

ANGELA: Are you both okay?

TITUS: We thought you were The Mouth Collector.

ANGELA: Oh thank goodness. Thank goodness you're both safe. Let's just go home, shall we? There's going to be another thunderstorm.

TITUS: Yeah, come on Miranda.

MIRANDA: No way am I going back to your weirdo house.

ANGELA: Please Miranda, it's just not safe –

MIRANDA: Don't even try and persuade me.

ANGELA: I know you're upset, but things can change.

TITUS: He'll be back any second!

ANGELA: We can sit down and talk. When I found Animal –

MIRANDA: Who wants to talk to a massive stupid cheat?!

ANGELA: When I found Animal –

MIRANDA: Shut up.

TITUS: Please!

ANGELA: I'll make things different.

MIRANDA: Yeah, with more bags of lies.

TITUS: So many lies, Mum.

ANGELA: If you give me a chance –

MIRANDA: I've given you a million chances!

ANGELA: But I promise.

MIRANDA: Your promises count for about as much as a dead monkey round here! Because listen to me, all right. I am sick to absolute death of your stupid way of doing things. I am not a pea and I am not perfect and I do not need someone locking me up in a box! I hate your house and I hate your way of doing things, so why don't you leave me alone?! Go on, get lost, you don't even flipping well like me! Making me do things I hate for the fun of it. Telling me lies for the fun of it. So just get out of my home!

(*She throws an apple at ANGELA.*)

Go, I said! Can't you hear me?!

(*She throws another apple.*)

Get out of my home, I said!

(*She picks up the picture frame to throw.*)

I hate your rules and I hate your lies and I hate…!

(*MIRANDA wants to say 'you' and throw the picture frame but can't. She shows ANGELA the picture.*)

Why can't things be more like the picture? My life used to be good like the picture. Why can't things be more like the picture?

(*MIRANDA lies face down on the floor, exhausted and tearful, clutching the picture. ANGELA and TITUS curl on top of her comfortingly. They are like a snug family of cats.*)

ANGELA: Let's try then. Let's try for that.

(*Pause.*)

TITUS: Maybe we should go now.

(*They uncurl and ANGELA helps MIRANDA up.*)

ANGELA: Let's get this one home, shall we? Into the warm. Titus, would you like to carry Animal?

(*TITUS looks down at the rucksack. ANGELA and MIRANDA head off.*)

TITUS: What's he doing out of his cage? Hey Mum, have you seen his fur?! And his eyes don't look scratched up any more. The illness must have gone! Come on, old boy.

(*TITUS puts the rucksack on his back.*)

Flip me, he weighs a ton.

(*TITUS leaves…*)

Hey Mum, I was dead brave earlier…

(*Short pause. THE MOUTH COLLECTOR comes back into the space. He seems more timid than before. He checks that TITUS and MIRANDA have gone. He sees the picture on the floor. He picks it up and looks at it, gently lays it on the top of a tree stump and rests his head on it.*)

SCENE FOUR

(*ANGELA, TITUS and MIRANDA are back at home. MIRANDA is painting over some of the rules. ANGELA is trying to pull TITUS' mask off.*)

ANGELA: Keep still.

TITUS: Owwwww! You're hurting me.

ANGELA: I'm doing my best.

TITUS: Your nails are digging into my neck.

ANGELA: What did you do to make it so stuck?

TITUS: Get it off. I can hardly breathe.

ANGELA: Perhaps some custard might make it more slippery.

TITUS: We finished the custard last night. On the banana cake.

ANGELA: Of course we did. Miranda, will you help me wrench it off? I think your strength might make the difference. You grab the mask and I'll grab his feet, then on my command we'll pull.

(*MIRANDA grabs the mask. ANGELA grabs his feet.*)

Have you got a good grip?

TITUS: Wait wait wait! This sounds a bit drastic. I value my ears, you know.

ANGELA: I'll count down from three.

TITUS: Hang on! What about olive oil?! What about egg whites?!

ANGELA: Three.

TITUS: Please.

ANGELA: Two.

TITUS: Try to be gentle.

ANGELA: One.

TITUS: I feel dizzy.

ANGELA: PULL!!!

> (*They pull. TITUS yells. The mask comes away. He continues yelling for a few seconds, then checks that all of his facial features are still attached to his head.*)

TITUS: That didn't hurt as much as I thought it would.

ANGELA: Good. Now, sit down and I'll serve up the kippers.

TITUS: Kippers?! Oh wow! Kippers, Miranda!

MIRANDA: What about the lobster claws? You said that if we had fish for breakfast we'd grow claws –

ANGELA: Yes, I'm sorry. We'll paint over that one.

TITUS: I was wondering what that smoky smell was!

ANGELA: Come and sit down.

> (*TITUS and MIRANDA sit at the table. ANGELA serves.*)

Kippers for Titus. Kippers for Miranda. Kipper for me.

> (*ANGELA sits. TITUS takes the salt, MIRANDA the pepper and ANGELA the vinegar. ANGELA and TITUS glance to MIRANDA, unsure as to whether to do the condiment ritual. She smiles.*)

TITUS: Salt!

MIRANDA: Pepper!

ANGELA: Vinegar!

> (*Switch.*)

TITUS: Pepper!

MIRANDA: Vinegar!

ANGELA: Salt!

> (*Switch.*)

TITUS: Vinegar!

MIRANDA: Salt!

ANGELA: Pepper!

>*(ANGELA closes her eyes and rests her fingers on her nose.)*

>Thank you for the tasty plate of kippers we're about to eat… Let's just get stuck in, shall we?

>*(They eat. Gradually, unnoticed by them, their hands turn into lobster claws.)*

TITUS: My head feels like a feather without that mask stuck on it. I hardly slept a wink.

MIRANDA: That's funny, you were snoring like an earthquake.

TITUS: I do not snore.

MIRANDA: I had to stuff socks in my ears.

TITUS: At least when I eat, I don't make squelching noises.

ANGELA: Before Titus' father died, every day would start with a kipper.

>*(Pause.)*

MIRANDA: Can I give some kipper to Animal?

ANGELA: Why? Don't you like it?

MIRANDA: I just think he might like it.

>*(ANGELA forces a smile in agreement. MIRANDA goes to feed Animal.)*

TITUS: I'm going to start a new painting today. A massive blue guinea pig playing a guitar.

MIRANDA: He loves it! He almost bit my hand off!

ANGELA: Dear old Animal.

MIRANDA: That scab is definitely smaller.

TITUS: And a squirrel on the piano in the background.

>*(MIRANDA comes back to the table. Pause.)*

ANGELA: What colour paint shall I buy for the walls?

TITUS: Red. No, indigo. No, orange and black stripes.

MIRANDA: I think you should paint them honey-coloured.

>*(Pause.)*

>Pass the pepper.

>*(TITUS passes the pepper. MIRANDA points at his hand.)*

119

Titus! Your hands! They've turned into claws!

TITUS: Oh my…! So have yours!

(*MIRANDA lets out a stifled scream.*)

Mum?

(*ANGELA slowly lifts her hands to reveal more claws. They stare at each other's claws, amazed. Animal has lobster claws too. They all hold their own claws up to the light and inspect them in a fascinated and flabbergasted way.*

END.)

APPENDIX

THE HOUSE SHOULD BE DECORATED WITH SOME OR ALL OF THE FOLLOWING RULES:

No squinting at the kitchen floor.

No skidding on the kitchen floor.

No handstands in the kitchen.

No bare feet in the kitchen.

No climbing into the refrigerator.

No standing on chairs.

No standing on tables.

No elbows on the table.

No juggling with fruit.

No wasting juice.

No making mixtures.

No fiddling with paper clips.

Don't stand too near the microwave.

Sheets must be washed on Saturdays.

Don't lean against the washing machine.

Don't breathe against the window.

Never open the window before midday.

Don't press your face against the window.

Don't sniff too much.

No imagining of future events.

No quacking like ducks.

No throwing of knives.

No opening sleeping people's eyes.

No pillow fights.

Hold your breath for 30 seconds at 3.00pm.

Cross your legs at 6.19pm.

No cheese before bed.

No pulling about of other people's faces.

No hitting, pinching or scratching.

No caterwauling or howling.

All singing must be gentle.

Only French must be spoken on Tuesday afternoons.

No pretending to be caterpillars.

No encouraging of cats.

Absolutely no kissing of dogs.

No setting fire to things.

No tramping over the pea patch.

Don't stamp in puddles or mud.

No jumping in high winds.

No sunbathing under tennis rackets.

No teetering on curbs or walls.

No putting glue on your hands then picking it off.

Glitter must be used sparingly.

No messing with clingfilm.

No highlighter pens.

No chucking sultanas about.

No pretending to be dead or asleep.

No chewing of gum whatsoever.

No pretending to chew gum.

No pretending to smoke.

No shouting 'penguin' at nuns.

The sink must be swilled after use.

No fake mice.

No giggling at strangers.

No spinning round and getting dizzy.

Shoes must be polished on Tuesdays.

Christmas presents must be opened on Boxing Day.

No kneeling on slippers.

No nursing poorly birds or bats.

Never open Animal's cage.

Animal's special diet must be strictly stuck to.

No whistling with fingers.

No exaggerated sneezes.

Scarves must travel twice around the neck.

Wipe the bath with the soft green cloth.

Wipe the toilet with the harsh red cloth.

Itching powder is strictly forbidden.

No badges.

No boxing or wrestling.

Teeth must be flossed on Sunday mornings.

No wearing watches round your ankles.

No pretending your fingers are guns.

No accumulating lolly-sticks.

No crunching ice in your mouth.

No hoarding of biscuits.

Rules for breakfast:

Breakfast must be eaten with a large plastic spoon.

Breakfast must consist of peas and only peas.

No making up songs about breakfast.

No pretending your peas are an army.

No pushing peas about your plate.

No putting peas in pictures, patterns or lines.

No speaking on behalf of peas.

No banging of plastic spoons.

No spilling.

No yawning.

No salt without pepper.

No swallowing without chewing.

No flicking.

Rules for mopping:
No pretending your mop is a snooker cue.
Mackintoshes must be worn.
No pretending your mop is a microphone.
No shoving mops into other people's faces.
One scoop of soap per bucket.
One mop per person.
No scrapping or skidding.
No pretend sword-fighting with mops.

A – Z OF RULES (ON THE CHILDREN'S BEDROOM WALL)

Animal's teeth must be brushed bi-annually.

Books must be about nice things.

Cats must be stroked the right way.

Dusting must be done in darkness.

Elbows must be scrubbed on Sundays.

Faces should not reast on hands.

Games must be played sportingly.

Hats must be of a single colour.

Insects must not be kept in tins.

Juice must be drunk through a straw.

Karate chopping is not allowed.

Light switches must not be used as toys.

Monkey noises are not allowed.

Nattering at bedtime is forbidden.

Old people must be smiled at.

Polish your Wellingtons monthly.

Quacking is forbidden.

Rolling balls about is not allowed.

Squealing is not permitted.

Tables and chairs must be treated with care.

Ulcers must be dabbed with ketchup.

Voices should not be raised.

Worms should not be forced to swim.

Xylophone practice must be on Tuesday.

Yoghurt must stay in the kitchen.

Zebras must never be mentioned.